150 Years of Magic

Over 150 irresistible classic and new recipes!

Years
of Magic

Editor: Mardi Edelstein

Writer: Karla Goldstein

Coordination: Moongate Publishing Inc.

Graphic Design: Lucie Benoit

Production: David Vanden; Monique Liboiron

Photography: Michael Alberstat; Douglas Bradshaw; Christopher Campbell; Peter Chou;
                    Yvonne Duivenvoorden; Colin Erricson; Rob Fiocca; Gad Foltys; Chris Freeland;
                    Bill Milne; Edward Pond; Paul Rosario, Rob Watson; Robert Wigington

Library and Archives Canada Cataloguing in Publication
150 Years of Magic / Eagle Family Foods Inc.
Issued also in French under title: 150 ans de magie.
ISBN 0-9781711-0-1
1. Desserts. I. Eagle Family Foods Inc. II. Title: One hundred and fifty years of magic.
TX773.064 2006
C2006-905046-5

Published in Canada by Moongate Publishing Inc.
Printed in Canada, Third quarter 2006.

Table of Contents

The Magic Ingredient

Smooth Silky Rich Creamy Dreamy Velvety ... just a few of the many words used to describe the miracle product invented by Gail Borden 150 years ago.

The Dessert Maker – The Most Trusted – The Original – The One and Only ... Quick and Easy – Fool-Proof – Quick Scratch – Pastry-Chef Quality – Versatile – Convenient – it's praises have been sung for more than 6 generations of bakers, who have given Eagle Brand the distinction of being The Magic Ingredient.

The magic started with a mission. After witnessing severe malnutrition in infants and children on long, arduous overseas voyages, it was inventor Gail Borden's idea to condense whole fresh milk in order to prolong its shelf life, make it safe and make it available where it wasn't readily accessible. Borden adapted a vacuum process used by the Shakers to remove most of the water from fresh milk he personally collected from local farmers, then added sugar for better preservation and taste. The result? The thick, sweet and decadent creamy delight we all know as Eagle Brand sweetened condensed milk.

From the time it was used as a coffee additive in Civil War rations through the years where refrigeration was in short supply, word spread of the milk that lasted indefinitely. Borden adopted the Eagle as his symbol of highest quality, to discern his product from the many imitators that sprung up after his success. Having heard that homemakers were finding new uses for Eagle Brand, in 1931 the Borden kitchens offered $25 for every original Eagle Brand recipe submitted. The response was astounding – over 38,000 women sent in over 81,000 recipes. Instantly a community of Eagle Brand bakers was born. The discoveries were endless.

Add hot water – It's a creamy smooth sauce. Melt with chocolate, add a bit of hot water – it's a dreamy frosting. With more hot water – it makes perfect hot chocolate. Melt with lots of chocolate – you get fudge and truffles - without a candy thermometer, and in mere minutes. With eggs you can whip up creamy puddings and custard fillings. Add lemon juice to Eagle Brand – and presto - a thick rich, and tangy mixture that sets up for pie fillings, mousses and trifles - without cooking. Boil Eagle Brand to create rich and creamy caramel of any consistency. Combine with whipped cream and freeze – you have ice cream, with no cooking and no ice cream maker. Mix it with icing sugar and flavouring – you've made fondant-like candy filling. And so, these early inventions revolutionized the kitchens of the modern post-war homemaker. Now, no-bake cheesecakes, brownies and refrigerator cakes, custards, rice puddings, "magic" lemon meringue pie and layered cookie bars were attainable anytime, in a fraction of the time it took their mothers and grandmothers to make Sunday dessert.

The *magic* of Eagle Brand is that it is not only a product, but a method of baking. Since it has already been pre-cooked and blended, preparation time is dramatically shortened, and consistent results guaranteed. That is why even the most novice of bakers can turn out an elegant pastry-chef quality creation in under 15 minutes. And that's why we say that it is a modern product for the modern traditionalist – of any decade.

since 1856

True to its original gold-standard formula, Eagle Brand has endured to this day because of its dedicated community of bakers. Countless stories have been shared via **Eagle Brand's Recipe Club** – touching and inspirational – from ordinary people who find strength and hope in good times and bad – through love of family, community, tradition and passing on the love of baking. Eagle Brand, considered the oldest food product brand name still in use, is like a family member or a trusted old friend lending familiarity and comfort to such important occasions as birthdays, anniversaries, fall bake sales, community fundraisers, pot luck suppers, and especially holiday dinners. Through it all, Gail Borden's original vision of quality, convenience and his passion for improving daily life has endured… and what greater measure of success could a magic ingredient wish for?

Elsie the Cow

What can we say about Elsie the Cow…? In the 1930's when The Borden Company adopted the now familiar aproned and daisy-festooned cartoon Elsie as its corporate mascot, it had no idea how popular and adored she would become.

By the late 1920's, The Borden Company had established itself as the frontrunner in the dairy industry. To promote itself at the 1939 New York World's Fair, it created an elaborate and ultra-modern exhibit featuring the "Rotolactor" - a futuristic-looking automated milking machine which could draw milk from 50 cows simultaneously. A huge audience gathered twice daily to watch this modern marvel, where an overwhelming number specifically asked which cow was Elsie! Up until then, Elsie had only existed as a cartoon character in a series of magazine ads for Borden milk.

A quick-thinking executive scoured Borden's herd of 150 pedigreed cows, and chose one wistful-eyed Jersey unusually named "You'll Do Lobelia" to play the role. She was quickly renamed Elsie, put on the Rotolactor between milkings, and suddenly the cartoon had a living, breathing counterpart that visitors immediately fell in love with. By the time the fair closed in 1940, *live* Elsie had become the #1 attraction! After the fair, the Elsie legacy sprouted a family. With husband Elmer and daughter Beulah now at her side, the traveling family act toured the country attracting huge crowds in their own personalized truck dubbed the "Cowdillac". On her own, Elsie enjoyed celebrity on a different scale, starring as "Buttercup" in the feature film "Little Men", and appearing at press dinners in swank New York nightclubs.

In 1941 the original Elsie was put to sleep after a truck accident. A new Elsie was quietly christened, and the public persona of the now-famous spokescow continued, as did her lineage. In the late 1940's Elsie gave birth to a brother for Beulah, named Beauregard, and in the 1950's twins Larabee and Lobelia were born. In the 1940's and 50's, hundreds of Elsie collectibles were manufactured – everything from clocks to jewelry, plush toys to sundae dishes. Elsie had emerged as a true icon, representing all that is wholesome, traditional and homemade; and was in her time, the most recognized and beloved advertising symbol in the world.

ELSIE

Bars & Cookies

*This #1 baking category features **Eagle Brand**® magic at its best and easiest. From layered bars to drop cookies, creamy cheesecake bars to moist and chewy brownies, classic coconut macaroons to super easy Skor® Bars - these versatile treats are perfect for lunch bags, after school snacks, holiday cookie swaps, bake sales, school fairs, picnics, entertaining, gift-giving, video night or…just because.*

*The most popular recipe in **Eagle Brand**® history, the one-pan Magic Cookie Bar debuted in the 1960's as the Hello Dolly. Forty years and an abundance of variations later, the Magic Bar still ranks no. 1 with busy mothers whose kids not only gobble them up, but love to make them as well!*

We have chosen a variety of classic and new bar and cookie recipes to help you make sweet memories for your family and friends. All in 1-2-3 easy steps!

The Original Magic Cookie Bar

The most popular recipe in Eagle Brand® history, this easy one-pan treat debuted in the 1960s as the "Hello Dolly". A multitude of variations have sprung up over the years… why not try some of your own!

PREP TIME: 8 minutes plus baking time
SERVINGS: 24 bars

2 cups (500 mL) graham crumbs
3/4 cup (175 mL) butter, melted
1 can (300 mL) **Regular
or Low Fat Eagle Brand**®
1 1/3 cups (325 mL) chopped pecans
1 1/3 cups (325 mL) semi-sweet
chocolate chips
1 1/3 cups (325 mL) sweetened
flaked coconut

1 Combine graham crumbs with butter; press evenly onto parchment paper-lined 13 x 9-inch (3.5 L) baking pan.

2 Pour Eagle Brand evenly over crumb crust.

3 Sprinkle with pecans, chocolate chips and coconut; press down firmly.

4 Bake in preheated 350°F (180°C) oven for 25 to 30 minutes or until lightly browned. Cool thoroughly and cut into bars. Store loosely covered at room temperature.

7 Layer Magic Cookie Bar:

Add 1 cup (250 mL) butterscotch chips to toppings.

Heavenly White Choc Toffee Bar:

Use as toppings: 1 pkg (225 g) white chocolate chips, 1 cup (250 mL) sweetened flaked coconut, 1/2 cup (125 mL) sliced almonds, toasted, and 3/4 cup (175 mL) toffee bits**

** may contain almonds

TIP:

Line your baking pan with parchment paper to 1-2" (2.5-5 cm) above the rim for even baking and to remove bars easily. It also makes clean-up a snap!

Pistachio Magic Cookie Bars

2 cups (500 mL) graham crumbs
3/4 cup (175 mL) butter, melted
1 can (300 mL) **Regular or Low Fat Eagle Brand**®
3/4 cup (175 mL) coarsely chopped hazelnuts
3/4 cup (175 mL) coarsely chopped pistachios
1 cup (250 mL) milk or semi-sweet chocolate chips
1/2 cup (125 mL) toffee bits

1 Combine graham crumbs with butter; press evenly onto parchment paper-lined 13 x 9-inch (3.5 L) baking pan.

2 Pour Eagle Brand evenly over crumb crust.

3 Sprinkle with nuts, chips and toffee bits; press down firmly.

4 Bake in preheated oven 250°F (125°C) 45-50 minutes, or until lightly browned. Cool thoroughly and cut into bars.

PREP TIME: 10 minutes
plus baking time
SERVINGS: 24 bars

Choco Banana Magic Bars

2 cups (500 mL) graham crumbs
3/4 cup (175 mL) butter, melted
1 can (300 mL) **Regular or Low Fat Eagle Brand**®
2 medium-sized bananas, mashed
1 1/2 cups (375 mL) semi-sweet chocolate chunks
1 cup (250 mL) flaked coconut
1 1/2 cups (375 mL) chopped pecans

1 Combine graham crumbs with butter; press evenly onto parchment paper-lined 13 x 9" (3.5 L) baking pan.

2 Combine Eagle Brand and bananas; pour evenly over crumb crust.

3 Top with chocolate, coconut and pecans; press down firmly.

4 Bake in preheated 350°F (180°C) oven for 20-25 minutes or until lightly browned. Cool thoroughly and cut into bars.

PREP TIME: 15 minutes
plus baking time
SERVINGS: 24 bars

Bars & Cookies

TIP:
If using a glass pan, reduce baking temperatures by 25°C (20°C)

Harvest Magic Bars

PREP TIME: 10 minutes
plus baking time
SERVINGS: 24 bars

2 cups (500 mL) graham crumbs
3/4 cup (175 mL) butter, melted
1 can (300 mL) **Regular or Low Fat Eagle Brand®**
1 pkg (225 g) white chocolate chips
3/4 cup (175 mL) each: dried cranberries and finely
   chopped dried apricots

1 Combine graham crumbs with butter; press evenly
onto parchment paper-lined 13 x 9 inch (3.5 L)
baking pan.

2 Pour Eagle Brand evenly over crumb crust.

3 Top with chocolate chips, cranberries and apricots;
press down firmly.

4 Bake in preheated 350°F (180°C) oven 20-25
minutes or until edges become lightly browned.
Cool thoroughly and cut into bars.

Magic Santa Cookie Bars

PREP TIME: 10 minutes
plus baking time
SERVINGS: 24 bars

2 cups (500 mL) graham crumbs
3/4 cup (175 mL) butter, melted
1 can (300 mL) **Regular or Low Fat Eagle Brand®**
1/2 cup (125 mL) chopped pecans
3/4 cups (175 mL) white or semi-sweet chocolate chips
1 cup (250 mL) dried cranberries
1 cup (250 mL) flaked coconut
1 cup (250 mL) mini-marshmallows

1 Combine graham crumbs with butter; press evenly
onto parchment paper-lined 13x9-inch (3.5 L)
baking pan.

2 Pour 2/3 Eagle Brand over crumbs.

3 Sprinkle with pecans, chips, cranberries, coconut and
marshmallows; press down firmly. Pour remaining
Eagle Brand overtop.

4 Bake in preheated 350°F (180°C) oven for 25 to
30 minutes or until lightly browned. Cool thoroughly
and cut into bars.

Magic Mallow Bars

PREP TIME: 10 minutes plus baking time
SERVINGS: 24 bars

2 cups (500 mL) graham crumbs
1 cup (250 mL) chopped peanuts
3/4 cup (175 mL) butter, melted
1 cup (250 mL) milk chocolate chips
1 cup (250 mL) peanut butter chips
2 1/2 cups (625 mL) miniature
  marshmallows
1 can (300 mL) **Regular or
Low Fat Eagle Brand®**
1/2 cup (125 mL) milk chocolate
  chips, melted

1 Combine crumbs, peanuts and butter; press evenly onto parchment paper-lined 13x9" (3.5 L) baking pan.

2 Layer milk chocolate chips, peanut butter chips and marshmallows over crust. Drizzle Eagle Brand evenly over all.

3 Bake in preheated 350°F(180°C) oven for 18-20 minutes or until golden brown. Cool.

4 Drizzle with melted milk chocolate chips. Cool thoroughly and cut into bars.

TIP:
When using marshmallows in a bar, pour Eagle Brand overtop to prevent marshmallows from burning.

Chocolate Maple Nut Bars

PREP TIME: 15 minutes
plus baking time
SERVINGS: 24 bars

1 1/2 cups (375 mL) unsifted flour
2/3 cup (150 mL) sugar
1/2 tsp (2.5 mL) salt
3/4 cup (175 mL) cold butter
2 eggs
1 can (300 mL) **Regular or Low Fat Eagle Brand®**
1 1/2 tsp (7mL) maple extract
2 cups (500 mL) chopped nuts
1 cup (250 mL) semi-sweet chocolate chips

1 Combine flour, sugar and salt; cut in butter until crumbly. Stir in 1 beaten egg. Press firmly on bottom of parchment paper-lined 13 x 9-inch (3.5 L) baking pan. Bake in preheated oven 350°F (180°C) 25 minutes.

2 In medium bowl, beat Eagle Brand, remaining egg and maple extract; stir in nuts.

3 Sprinkle chocolate chips evenly over baked crust. Top with Eagle Brand mixture; bake 25 minutes longer or until golden. Cool thoroughly and chill. Cut into bars. Store tightly.

Mochaccino Nut Bars

Substitute 2-3 tbsp (30-45 mL) cold, strong coffee and 1 tsp (5 mL) vanilla extract for maple extract in Step 2.

Butterscotch Apple Magic Bars

PREP TIME: 8 minutes
plus baking time
SERVINGS: 24 bars

2 cups (500 mL) graham wafer crumbs
3/4 cup (175 mL) butter, melted
1 can (300 mL) **Regular or Low Fat Eagle Brand®**
1 1/4 cups (300 mL) chopped fresh or dried apples
1 1/4 cups (300 mL) chopped pecans
1 1/4 cups (300 mL) butterscotch chips

1 Combine graham crumbs with butter; press evenly onto parchment paper-lined 13 x 9-inch (3.5 L) baking pan.

2 Pour Eagle Brand evenly over crumbs. Sprinkle with dried apples, pecans and chips; press down firmly.

3 Bake in preheated 350°F (180°C) oven for 25 to 30 minutes or until lightly browned. Cool thoroughly and cut into bars.

Crunchy Lemon Squares

PREP TIME: 15 minutes plus baking time
SERVINGS: 9 3-inch squares or 18 smaller bars

1 cup (250 mL) quick oats, uncooked
1 cup (250 mL) flour
1/2 cup (125 mL) flaked coconut
1/2 cup (125 mL) coarsely chopped walnuts
1/2 cup (125 mL) firmly-packed light brown sugar
1 tsp (5 mL) baking powder
1/2 cup (125 mL) butter, melted
1 can (300 mL) **Regular or Low Fat Eagle Brand**®
1/2 cup (125 mL) lemon juice
1 tbsp (15 mL) grated lemon rind

1 Combine oats, flour, coconut, nuts, sugar, baking powder, and butter until crumbly. Pat 1/2 of crumb mixture evenly on bottom of 9 x 9-inch (3 L) parchment paper-lined baking pan. Reserve other half.

2 In medium bowl, combine Eagle Brand, lemon juice, and rind. Pour mixture onto crumb layer. Sprinkle remaining crumb mixture on top.

3 Bake in preheated 350°F (180°C) oven 25 to 30 minutes. Cool thoroughly and cut into squares.

Bars & Cookies

TIP:
Eagle Brand thickens "magically" when its pre-cooked blend of milk and sugar is combined with an acid ingredient such as lemon, orange or chocolate, allowing it to create creamy no-bake puddings, pie fillings, frozen desserts, and sauces.

Oatmeal Fudge Bars

PREP TIME: 15 minutes
plus baking time
SERVINGS: 24 bars

2 cups (500 mL) brown sugar
1 cup (250 mL) butter
2 eggs
1 tsp (5 mL) vanilla
1 tsp (5 mL) baking soda
2 1/4 cups (550 mL) all-purpose flour
3 cups (750 mL) quick cooking oatmeal
1 cup (250 mL) chopped nuts (optional)
2 cups (500 mL) semi-sweet or milk chocolate chips
1 can (300 mL) **Regular or Low Fat Eagle Brand**®
2 tbsp (30 mL) butter

1 Cream together brown sugar and 1 cup (250 mL) butter. Beat in eggs and vanilla. Add baking soda, flour and oatmeal and nuts, if using, and combine well. Pat 2/3 of oatmeal mixture into a parchment paper-lined 9x13-inch (3.5 L) baking pan.

2 Melt chocolate chips with Eagle Brand and butter. Pour over base. Drop reserved oatmeal mixture by rounded teaspoonfuls onto chocolate mixture.

3 Bake in preheated 350°F (180°C) oven 20-25 minutes or until golden brown. Let cool for 10 minutes and cut into bars while still warm.

Chocolate Crunch Bars

PREP TIME: 10 minutes
plus baking time
SERVINGS: 16 bars

4 cups (1 L) toasted rice cereal
1 cup (250 mL) semi-sweet chocolate chips
1/2 cup (125 mL) chopped toasted almonds
1/2 cup (125 mL) flaked coconut
1 can (300 mL) **Regular or Low Fat Eagle Brand**®
3/4 cup (175 mL) candy-coated chocolate pieces

1 Combine cereal, chocolate chips, almonds and coconut. Add Eagle Brand and mix until well combined. Spread mixture into parchment paper-lined 8-inch (2 L) square baking pan.

2 Bake in preheated 350°F (180°C) oven for 20 to 25 minutes or until just golden.

3 Press candy pieces into top while still warm. Cool thoroughly and cut into bars.

Skor Bars

PREP TIME: 6 minutes plus baking time
SERVINGS: 16 bars

1 pkg (250 g) Ritz® Crackers
1/2 cup (125 mL) Skor® toffee bits*
1 can (300 mL) **Regular
or Low Fat Eagle Brand**®

*contain chopped almonds

1 Finely crush crackers. Add Skor toffee bits and Eagle Brand, mixing until fully blended.

2 Pour into 9x9" parchment paper-lined baking pan. Bake in preheated 350°F (180°C) oven for 18-20 minutes. Let cool. Cut into squares.

Chocolate Chip Skor Bars:

Fold in 1/2 cup (125 mL) semi-sweet or milk chocolate chips to mixture.

Chocolate Skor Bars :

Combine Eagle Brand and 1/2 cup (125 mL) unsweetened cocoa. Add toffee bits and crushed crackers. Bake as above.

®Ritz Crackers is a trademark of Kraft Foods Global, Inc.
®SKOR is a trademark of Hershey Chocolate & Confectionary Corp.

TIP:
For a quick and clean way to make cracker or cookie crumbs, place in a large resealable plastic storage bag, press out air, seal, then crush with rolling pin.

Eagle Brand Fudge Brownies

Classic

Eagle Brand has been making "child's play" out of brownies for generations. Try these variations, or make up some of your own

PREP TIME: 10 minutes plus baking time
SERVINGS: 24 brownies

8 squares (1oz/28g each) semi-sweet
  or milk chocolate, divided
1/4 cup (50 mL) butter
2 cups (500 mL) biscuit baking mix
1 can (300 mL) **Regular or
  Low Fat Eagle Brand**®
1 egg, beaten
1 tsp (5 mL) vanilla extract
1 cup (250 mL) chopped nuts
  (optional)

1 Melt 4 squares of semi-sweet chocolate with butter; remove from heat. Add baking mix, Eagle Brand, egg and vanilla. Mix well.

2 Chop remaining chocolate and stir into mixture. Pour into greased 9-inch (23 cm) square pan. Top with nuts.

3 Bake at 350°F (180°C) for 25-30 minutes. Cool. Cut into squares.

Mint Chocolate Brownies:

Substitute 1 cup (250 mL) mint chocolate chips for 4 squares of semi-sweet chocolate. Omit vanilla extract.

Chocolate Orange Brownies:

Add 1-2 tsp (5-10 mL) grated orange rind in Step 2. Omit vanilla extract.

Cookie Crunch Brownies:

Stir in 2/3 cup (175 mL) of your favourite cookie, chopped (Chocolate chip, Crème sandwich cookie, Vanilla wafer, Peanut Butter)

Brownie Cheesecake Bars

1 pkg (24 oz/ 680 g) fudge brownie mix
1 cup (250 mL) chopped nuts (optional)
1 pkg (250 g) cream cheese, softened
2 tbsp (30 mL) butter, softened
1 tbsp (15 mL) cornstarch
1 can (300 mL) **Regular or Low Fat Eagle Brand**®
1 egg
2 tsp (10 mL) vanilla extract
2 squares (28 g each) semi-sweet chocolate, melted

1 Prepare brownie mix as package directs. Stir in nuts, if desired. Spread into parchment paper-lined 13x9-inch (3.5 L) baking pan.

2 With mixer, beat cream cheese, butter and cornstarch in large bowl until fluffy. Gradually beat in Eagle Brand. Add egg and vanilla; beat until smooth. Pour cheesecake mixture evenly over brownie batter.

3 Bake in preheated 350°F (180°C) oven 40 minutes or until top is lightly browned. Cool. Drizzle with melted chocolate. Chill. Cut into bars.

PREP TIME: 20 minutes
plus baking time
SERVINGS: 24-36 bars

No-Bake Fudgy Brownies

1 can (300 mL) **Regular or Low Fat Eagle Brand**®
2 squares (1 oz/28 g each) unsweetened chocolate, coarsely chopped
1 tsp (5 mL) vanilla extract
2 cups plus 2 tbsp (530 mL) packaged chocolate cookie crumbs
1/4 cup (50 mL) candy-coated milk chocolate candies or chopped nuts

1 Combine Eagle Brand and chocolate; cook and stir over low heat just until boiling. Cook and stir for 2 to 3 minutes more or until mixture thickens. Remove from heat.

2 Stir in vanilla. Stir in 2 cups (500 mL) cookie crumbs.

3 Spread evenly into parchment paper-lined 8-inch (2 L) square baking pan. Sprinkle with remaining cookie crumbs and candies or nuts; press down gently with back of spoon. Cover and chill for 4 hours or until firm. Cut into squares.

PREP TIME: 10 minutes
plus chilling time
SERVINGS: 1 dozen brownies

Bars & Cookies

Chewy Butterscotch Blondies

PREP TIME: 15 minutes plus baking time
SERVINGS: 20 bars

1/4 cup (50 mL) butter, melted
1 can (300 mL) **Regular or Low Fat Eagle Brand®**
1 egg
1 tsp (5 mL) vanilla
1 1/3 cups (325 mL) biscuit baking mix
1 tsp (5 mL) ground cinnamon
2/3 cup (150 mL) butterscotch-flavoured chips
2/3 cup (150 mL) chopped pecans or walnuts
1/2 cup (125 mL) unsweetened shredded coconut (optional)

1 Combine butter and Eagle Brand; stir in egg and vanilla. Mix well.

2 Reserving 2 tbsp (30 mL) biscuit mix, whisk remaining biscuit mix and cinnamon into Eagle Brand mixture, blending well.

3 Toss the reserved biscuit mix with butterscotch chips. Add chips, nuts and coconut into batter. Pour into parchment paper-lined 9x9-inch (2 L) pan.

4 Bake in preheated 350°F (180°C) oven 40 minutes or until golden brown and knife inserted in centre comes out clean. Cool; cut into bars.

What's a Blondie ?

Moist like brownies, cream-coloured blondies taste of brown sugar, butter and vanilla and spices, especially cinnamon or freshly grated nutmeg. Blondies go well in autumn with apple cider, mulled wine or hot coffee and in spring topped with vanilla or cinnamon ice cream !

Bars & Cookies

Bikini Bars *Classic*

The 1950's brought us Sunset Boulevard, early rock'n roll... and the Bikini Bar.

1 can (300 mL) **Regular or Low Fat Eagle Brand**®
1 tsp (5 mL) vanilla extract
Pinch salt
2 1/2 cups (625 mL) flaked coconut
2 cups (500 mL) chopped dates
2 cups (500 mL) chopped pecans
1/4 cup (50 mL) finely chopped maraschino cherries
1 cup (250 mL) butter icing
1/4 cup (50 mL) semi-sweet chocolate chips, melted

1 Blend together Eagle Brand, salt and vanilla. Stir in coconut, dates, pecans and cherries. Spoon mixture into 8" square (2 L) parchment paper-lined baking pan.

2 Bake in preheated 180°C (350°F) oven for 30 minutes; remove and let cool 2-3 minutes. Remove paper and cool completely. Spread butter icing over the cool bars and drizzle with melted chocolate. Let topping set. Cut into bars.

PREP TIME: 10 minutes plus baking time
SERVINGS: 24 bars

Top Hat Triple Layer Bars

1/2 cup (125 mL) butter, melted
1 1/2 cups (375 mL) graham wafer crumbs
1 pkg (200 g) flaked coconut
1 can (300 mL) **Regular or Low Fat Eagle Brand**®
1 pkg (350 g) semi-sweet chocolate chips
1/2 cup (125 mL) creamy peanut butter

1 Combine crumbs and melted butter; press into a parchment paper-lined 13 x 9 inch (3.5 L) baking pan.

2 Top evenly with coconut, then Eagle Brand.

3 Bake in preheated 350°F (180°C) oven 25 minutes or until lightly browned.

4 In small saucepan over low heat, melt chips with peanut butter. Spread evenly over hot coconut layer. Cool 30 minutes; chill. Remove parchment paper. Cut into bars.

PREP TIME: 20 minutes plus baking time
SERVINGS: 36 bars

Bars & Cookies

Chocolate Streusel Cream Cheese Bars

PREP TIME: 20 minutes plus baking time
SERVINGS: 24 to 36 bars

1 3/4 cups (425 mL) all-purpose flour
1 1/2 cups (375 mL) icing sugar
1/2 cup (125 mL) unsweetened cocoa
1 cup (250 mL) cold butter
1 pkg (250 g) cream cheese, softened
1 can (300 mL) **Regular or
Low Fat Eagle Brand**®
1 egg
2 tsp (10 mL) vanilla extract
1 cup (250 mL) fresh or frozen
raspberries, chopped (optional)
1/2 cup (125 mL) chopped walnuts
(optional)

1 Combine flour, sugar and cocoa; cut in butter until crumbly (mixture will be dry). Reserving 2 cups (500 mL) crumb mixture, press remainder firmly on bottom of 13 x 9-inch (3.5 L) parchment paper-lined baking pan. Bake in preheated oven 15 minutes.

2 Meanwhile beat cream cheese until fluffy. Gradually beat in Eagle Brand until smooth. Add egg and vanilla; mix well. Pour evenly over baked crust. Sprinkle raspberries over cream cheese mixture, if using.

3 Combine reserved crumb mixture with nuts if desired; sprinkle evenly over top. Bake 25 minutes or until bubbly. Cool. Chill. Cut into bars.

Lemon Nanaimo Bars

PREP TIME: 20 minutes plus baking and chilling time
SERVINGS: 24 bars

1/2 cup (125 mL) butter, melted
1/4 cup (50 mL) packed brown sugar
1/4 cup (50 mL) unsweetened
  cocoa powder
1 egg, beaten
2 cups (500 mL) graham wafer crumbs
1 cup (250 mL) flaked coconut
1/2 cup (125 mL) unsalted peanuts
  or walnuts, finely chopped
1 can (300 mL) **Regular or
  Low Fat Eagle Brand**® divided
2 – 2 1/2 cups (500-625 mL)
  icing sugar
1 tbsp (15 mL) custard powder
1/4 cup (50 mL) lemon juice
4 squares (1 oz/28 g each)
  semi-sweet chocolate, chopped

1 Combine melted butter, sugar, cocoa, egg, crumbs, coconut and nuts. Press evenly into bottom of a parchment paper-lined 9-inch (2.5 L) square pan. Bake in centre of preheated 350°F (180°C) oven for 10 minutes. Let cool.

2 Beat together half of Eagle Brand (150 mL) with sugar, custard powder, and lemon juice, until smooth and thick; spread evenly over base. Cover and refrigerate for about 2 hours or until chilled and set.

3 Melt chocolate with remaining Eagle Brand (150 mL), stirring until completely smooth. Spread evenly over base. Chill until firm. Cut into bars.

Snowy Coconut Macaroons

Classic

*Eagle Brand Snowy Macaroons have been a Christmas tradition for more than 60 years...
and they're Santa's favourite too!*

PREP TIME: 10 minutes plus baking time
SERVINGS: 4 dozen

1 can (300 mL) Regular Eagle
  Brand®
2 tsp (10 mL) vanilla extract
1 1/2 tsp (7 mL) almond extract
3 pkgs (200 g each) flaked coconut

1 Combine Eagle Brand, vanilla and
almond extracts and coconut; mix
well.

2 Place rounded spoonfuls onto well
greased cookie sheets.

3 Bake 12 at a time, on middle rack
of preheated 325°F (160°C) oven
10-12 minutes or until browned
around the edges. Remove
immediately to wire racks; cool
completely.

Macaroon Kisses (shown)

Upon removing from oven, immediately press candy
kiss in centre of each macaroon.

Chocolate Macaroons

Omit almond extract. Add 4 squares (1 oz/28 g
each) unsweetened chocolate, melted to Step 1.

Chocolate Chip Macaroons

Omit almond extract. Fold in 1 cup (250 mL) mini
chocolate chips in Step 1.

Coffee Almond Macaroons

Add 3 tbsp (45 mL) cold strong coffee to Eagle
Brand. Stir in 1/2 cup (175 mL) slivered almonds,
toasted.

NOTE: 1 cup (250 mL) flaked coconut = 100 g of
any type of shredded coconut

TIP:

For best results with macaroons, we recommend a medium flaked sweetened coconut for optimum
binding. Don't drop, but shape them into rounded spoonfuls; pressing the mixture lightly together.

Bars & Cookies

Gingered Lemon Cookies

1 cup (250 mL) butter, softened
1 cup (250 mL) sugar
2 eggs
1 can (300 mL) **Regular or Low Fat Eagle Brand**®
4 tbsp (60 mL) lemon juice
2 tbsp (30 mL) grated lemon rind
2 tsp (10 mL) vanilla
1/3 cup (75 mL) finely chopped crystallized ginger
5 cups (1.25 L) all-purpose flour
4 tsp (20 mL) baking powder
1 tsp (5 mL) salt

1 Cream butter and sugar. Add the eggs, Eagle Brand, lemon juice, lemon rind and vanilla; mix until smooth. Fold in chopped ginger.

2 Sift together flour, baking powder and salt. Add to creamed mixture and mix well. Divide dough into 3 balls. Wrap in plastic and refrigerate 4 hours.

3 On floured surface, or between two pieces of parchment paper, roll each ball out to 1/4" (.5 cm) thick and cut into desired shapes.

4 Bake in preheated 350°F (180°C) oven for 10-12 minutes. Cool on a rack.

PREP TIME: 20 minutes
plus baking and chilling time
SERVINGS: 8 dozen cookies

Lemon Drizzle (optional)

Combine 1 1/2 cup (375 mL) sifted icing sugar, 4 tbsp (60 mL) water and 1 tbsp (15 mL) lemon juice; mix well.
Drizzle over cooled cookies.

Peanut Butter and Jelly Cookies

1 can (300 mL) **Regular or Low Fat Eagle Brand**®
1 cup (250 mL) smooth peanut butter
1 egg
2 tsp (10 mL) vanilla extract
2 cups (500 mL) all-purpose flour
1 tsp (5 mL) baking soda
1/4 tsp (1 mL) salt
Favourite variety of jelly or jam

1 Beat Eagle Brand with peanut butter, egg and vanilla until smooth. Mix in flour, baking soda and salt until well blended.

2 Shape into 1" (2.5 cm) balls. Place 2" (5 cm) apart on parchment paper-lined baking sheets. Press thumb in centre of each ball; fill with jelly or jam.

3 Bake in preheated 375°F (190°C) oven for 12 minutes or until lightly browned; transfer to rack to cool.

PREP TIME: 10 minutes
plus baking time
SERVINGS: about 40 cookies

Coconut Fingers *Classic*

Known in the late 1930's as "Depression Bars", after the era where sweets were a rarity and a great privilege!

PREP TIME: 15 minutes
plus baking time
SERVINGS: 48 fingers

12 slices white or whole wheat bread
   (day old best), crusts removed, if desired
1 can (300 mL) **Regular or Low Fat Eagle Brand**®
1 pkg (300 mL) flaked coconut

1 Cut bread into 4 strips (1/2-3/4" /1.2-3.75 cm wide).

2 Pour Eagle Brand 1/4 can (75 mL) at a time onto a large flat plate. Dip bread strips into Eagle Brand and then roll in coconut.

3 Bake in preheated 325°F (160°C) oven 8-10 minutes or until golden. Cool. Chill, if desired.

Pink tinted Coconut Fingers

Toss flaked coconut with a few drops of red food colouring in a bag or container. Proceed as above.

Chocolate Coconut Fingers

Combine 1 can (300 mL) Eagle Brand with 2 tbsp (30 mL) unsweetened cocoa powder (shown in picture).

Treasure Cookies

PREP TIME: 15 minutes
plus baking time
SERVINGS: about 2 dozen cookies.

1 1/2 cups (375 mL) graham crumbs
1/2 cup (125 mL) all-purpose flour
2 tsp (10 mL) baking powder
1 can (300 mL) **Regular or Low Fat Eagle Brand**®
1/2 cup (125 mL) butter, softened
1 cup (250 mL) flaked coconut
2 cups (500 mL) raisins
1 1/2 cups (375 mL) semi-sweet chocolate chunks
1 cup (250 mL) chopped pecans (optional)

1 Mix together graham crumbs, flour and baking powder; set aside.

2 Beat Eagle Brand and butter until smooth. Add graham crumb mixture; mix well. Stir in coconut, raisins, chocolate and pecans.

3 Drop by rounded tablespoonfuls onto parchment paper-lined cookie sheets.

4 Bake in preheated 375°F (190°C) oven for 9-10 minutes, or until lightly browned..

Decadent Double Chocolate Cookies

1 1/2 cups (375 mL) graham crumbs
2/3 cup (150 mL) all-purpose flour
1/4 cup (50 mL) cocoa powder
2 tsp (10 mL) baking powder
1 can (300 mL) **Regular or Low Fat Eagle Brand**®
1/2 cup (125 mL) butter, softened
6 oz (170 g) white chocolate, chopped
1 cup (250 mL) chopped pecans

1 Mix together graham crumbs, flour, cocoa powder and baking powder; set aside.

2 Beat Eagle Brand and butter until smooth. Add graham crumb mixture; mix well. Stir in white chocolate and pecans. Chill 30 minutes.

3 Drop by rounded tablespoonfuls onto parchment paper-lined baking sheets.

4 Bake in preheated oven 12-14 minutes; transfer to rack to cool.

PREP TIME: 10 minutes
plus chilling and baking time
SERVINGS: 40 cookies

Extra Energy Granola Bars

3 cups (750 mL) rolled oats
1 cup (250 mL) chopped nuts
1 cup (250 mL) raisins or chopped dried fruit
1 cup (250 mL) sunflower seeds
1 cup (250 mL) semi-sweet chocolate chips
   (optional)
1 can (300 ml) **Regular or Low Fat Eagle Brand**®
1/2 cup (125 mL) butter, melted

1 In large mixing bowl, combine all ingredients; mix well. Press evenly into a 15 X 10-inch (2 L) jelly roll pan lined with parchment paper.

2 Bake in preheated 325°F (160°F) oven for 25 to 30 minutes or until golden brown. Cool slightly; remove from pan and peel off paper. Cut into bars.

PREP TIME: 10 minutes
plus baking time
SERVINGS: 36 bars

Dainty Caramel Triangles

PREP TIME: 15 minutes
plus baking time
SERVINGS: 20 triangles

1 1/4 cups (300 mL) all-purpose flour
1/4 cup (50 mL) brown sugar
2/3 cup (150 mL) butter, softened and divided
1 can (300 mL) **Regular or Low Fat Eagle Brand**®
1/4 cup (50 mL) corn syrup
1/2 cup (125 mL) chopped semi-sweet chocolate
1/2 cup (125 mL) pecan halves

1 Combine flour and sugar; cut in 1/2 cup (125 mL) butter to form a soft dough. Press into parchment paper-lined 8-inch (2 L) square baking pan. Bake in preheated 350°F (180°C) oven 12-15 minutes or until lightly golden.

2 In saucepan, combine Eagle Brand, corn syrup and remaining butter. Cook over medium-low heat, stirring constantly until mixture turns a light caramel colour. Spread over warm crust.

3 Top at once with chocolate and pecans. Chill; cut into 20 triangles.

Holiday Jewel Triangles

PREP TIME: 10 minutes
plus baking time
SERVINGS: 2 1/2 dozen triangles

1/2 cup (125 mL) butter, softened
1/2 cup (125 mL) sugar
1 egg
1 tsp (5 mL) vanilla
2 1/4 cups (550 mL) all-purpose flour
1 can (300 mL) **Regular or Low Fat Eagle Brand**®
1/4 cup (50 mL) orange juice
1 1/4 cups (300 mL) chopped pecans
1 1/4 cups (300 mL) sweetened flaked coconut
2/3 cup each: (150 mL each) chopped red and green glacé cherries

1 Cream butter, sugar, egg and vanilla until light and creamy. Gradually add flour, mixing until crumbly. Press firmly onto parchment paper-lined 15 x 10 inch (2 L) jelly roll pan. Bake in preheated 350°F (180°C) oven for 5-6 minutes and set aside.

2 Stir together Eagle Brand, orange juice, pecans, coconut and cherries. Spread evenly over prepared crust.

3 Bake 20-25 minutes longer. Cool thoroughly and chill before cutting.

Bars & Cookies

Apple Cobblestone Cookies

PREP TIME: 10 minutes plus baking time
SERVINGS: about 4 dozen cookies

2 tbsp (30 mL) lemon juice
1 tbsp (15 mL) ground cinnamon
2 cups (500 mL) chopped dried apples
2 cups (500 mL) quick cooking oats
1/2 cup (125 mL) raisins
1/4 cup (50 mL) unsifted flour
1 can (300 mL) **Regular or
Low Fat Eagle Brand**®

1 In small bowl, sprinkle lemon juice and cinnamon over apples; toss. Set aside.

2 In large bowl, combine oats, raisins and flour. Add apple mixture and Eagle Brand; mix well. Drop by rounded teaspoonfuls onto parchment paper-lined baking sheets.

3 Bake in preheated 350°F (180°C) oven 8 to 10 minutes or until lightly browned. Remove from baking sheet. Cool.

Butterscotch Apple Cobblestones

Replace raisins with 1/2 cup (125 mL) butterscotch-flavoured chips.

TIP:

We recommend a slightly tart fall apple for baking, like Empire, Macintosh or Golden Delicious. Chop them with the skin on or off... your choice.

Cheesecakes, Cakes & Dessert Squares

Since the introduction of New York's most famous dessert in the 1960's, we have been in love with cheesecake, and Eagle Brand makes cheesecake with the creamiest texture imaginable. What used to just come in basic white with fruit toppings can now be enjoyed in such flavours as chocolate, hazelnut, mint and Black Forest, luscious caramel, tipsy rum'n eggnog and piña colada, tangy lemon and cranberry, and sweet and spicy pumpkin. Eagle Brand even makes no-bake and frozen cheesecakes - foolproof and fantastic in just minutes!

From the versatile Anniversary Cake to the sweet decadent Tres Leches, Eagle Brand has a moist and memorable cake for every occasion. And nobody makes holiday fruitcake "fast 'n fabulous" like Eagle Brand. For seasonal entertaining or gift-giving, this moist and hearty fruitcake is one of Eagle Brand's top 10 recipes of all time.

Enjoy the many flavours of sweet and sophisticated cakes and cheesecakes, with pastry chef results!

Truffle Cheesecake

Rich and fluffy... what dreams are made of !

PREP TIME: 15 minutes plus baking & chilling time
SERVINGS: 6-8

1 1/2 cups (375 mL) chocolate cookie crumbs

1/3 cup (75 mL) butter, melted

3 pkgs (250 g each) cream cheese, softened

1 can (300 mL) **Regular or Low Fat Eagle Brand**®

1 pkg (225 g) semi-sweet chocolate squares, melted

4 eggs

1/4 cup (50 mL) coffee-flavoured liqueur (optional)

2 tsp (10 mL) vanilla extract

1 Mix together cookie crumbs and butter. Press firmly onto bottom of 9" (23 cm) springform pan.

2 In large mixer bowl, beat cream cheese until fluffy. Gradually beat in Eagle Brand until smooth. Add remaining ingredients; mix well.

3 Pour into prepared pan.

4 Bake 1 hour in preheated 325°F (160°C) oven, or until centre is set. Cool, then chill 1 hour.

TIP:

Cracking in the top of a cheesecake is a result of over-baking. To prevent your cheesecake from cracking, check it 5 to 10 minutes before the end of the recommended baking time. Without touching the top of the cheesecake, lightly jiggle the pan to see if the centre looks firm.

Cranberry Cheesecake

1 cup (250 mL) graham crumbs
1/4 cup (50 mL) butter, melted
3 pkgs (250 g each) regular or light cream
   cheese, softened
1 can (300 mL) **Regular or Low Fat Eagle Brand**®
3 eggs
1 cup (250 mL) chopped fresh or frozen
   cranberries, thawed

1 Combine crumbs and butter; press onto bottom
of 9" (23 cm) springform pan.

2 Beat cream cheese until fluffy; gradually add Eagle
Brand and eggs. Stir in cranberries. Pour into prepared
pan.

3 Bake in preheated 325°F (160°C) oven for
45-50 minutes or until set. Cool thoroughly and chill
4 hours or overnight. Garnish as desired.

PREP TIME: 15 minutes
plus baking and chillimg time
SERVINGS: 10-12

Mini White Chocolate Cheesecakes

1 cup (250 mL) graham wafer crumbs
1/2 cup (125 mL) ground almonds
1/4 cup (50 mL) sugar
1/3 cup (75 mL) butter, melted
2 pkgs (250 g each) regular or light cream cheese,
   softened
1 can (300 mL) **Regular or Low Fat Eagle Brand**®
2 eggs
8 oz (225 g) white chocolate, melted

1 Combine crumbs, ground almonds, sugar and
butter; press equal portions firmly onto bottoms
of 24 paper-lined muffin cups.

2 Beat cream cheese until fluffy. Gradually add Eagle
Brand, eggs and white chocolate. Spoon equal
amounts of mixture into prepared cups.

3 Bake in preheated 300ºF (150ºC) oven for
16-18 minutes. Cool thoroughly and chill 4 hours
or overnight.

PREP TIME: 25 minutes
plus baking and chilling time
SERVINGS: 24 individual cheesecakes

Caramel Cheesecake

1 1/2 cups (375 mL) graham crumbs
1/2 cup (125 mL) butter, melted
1/2 cup (125 mL) caramel or butterscotch
  flavoured topping sauce
1 cup (250 mL) chopped pecans
3 pkgs (250 g each) regular or light cream cheese,
  softened
1 can (300 mL) **Regular or Low Fat Eagle Brand**®
3 eggs
1 tsp (5 mL) vanilla extract

1 Combine crumbs with butter. Press onto bottom and
halfway up sides of 9 " (23 cm) springform pan. Pour
caramel sauce over crust and top with pecans.

2 Beat cream cheese until fluffy. Gradually beat
in Eagle Brand, eggs and vanilla; pour over crust.

3 Bake in preheated 325°F (160°C) oven for
45-50 minutes or until centre is just set. Cool
thoroughly and chill 4 hours or overnight.

Lucky Mint Cheesecake

Yummy and minty and perfect for St. Patty's Day !

1/2 cup (125 mL) semi-sweet chocolate chips
1 can (300 mL) **Regular or Low Fat Eagle Brand**®
1 tsp (5 mL) vanilla extract
1 9 " (23 cm) ready-made chocolate crumb pie
  crust
1 pkg (250 g) cream cheese, softened
1/2 tsp (2.5 mL) mint extract
Several drops green food colouring
1 egg

1 Melt chips with 1/3 cup (75 mL) Eagle Brand. Stir in
vanilla. Spread mixture on bottom of pie crust.

2 Beat cream cheese until fluffy; gradually beat in remaining Eagle Brand, mint extract and green food colouring.
Add egg; beat on low speed just until combined. Pour
mint mixture over chocolate layer in pie crust.

3 Bake in preheated 350°F (180°C) oven 25 minutes
or until centre is just set. Cool thoroughly and chill 4
hours or overnight.

New York Cheesecake

PREP TIME: 15 minutes plus baking and chilling time
SERVINGS: 8-10

1 1/4 cups (300 mL) graham
  cracker crumbs
1/4 cup (50 mL) sugar
1/3 cup (75 mL) butter, melted
4 pkgs (250 g each) cream cheese,
  softened
1 can (300 mL) **Regular or
  Low Fat Eagle Brand**®
4 eggs
1/3 cup (75 mL) all-purpose flour
1 tbsp (15 mL) vanilla extract
1/2 tsp (2.5 mL) grated lemon rind
Fresh fruit or berries of choice:
OR
1 can (19 oz/540 mL) fruit pie filling
  of choice

1 Combine crumbs, sugar and butter; press firmly
onto bottom of 9″ (23 cm) springform pan.

2 Beat cream cheese until fluffy. Gradually beat in
Eagle Brand until smooth. Add eggs, flour, vanilla
and rind; mix well. Pour into prepared pan.

3 Bake in preheated 300°F (150°C) oven 1 hour or
until lightly browned. Cool thoroughly and chill 4
hours or overnight.

4 Before serving, top with fresh fruit or chilled
pie filling of choice.

TIP:

Cheesecakes can be frozen, tightly wrapped for 4-6 weeks, without glazes or toppings. Thaw 15-20
minutes at room temperature before adding glazes or toppings.

Triple Threat Chocolate Cheesecake

PREP TIME: 25 minutes plus baking and chilling time
SERVINGS: 8-10 portions

1 1/3 cups (325 mL) chocolate wafer crumbs

1/3 cup (75 mL) butter, melted

2 pkgs (250 g each) regular or light cream cheese, softened

1 can (300 mL) **Regular or Low Fat Eagle Brand**®

2 eggs

4 oz (114 g) white chocolate, melted

2 tbsp (30 mL) hazelnut or almond liqueur (optional)

4 oz (114 g) semi-sweet chocolate, melted

1/2 cup (125 mL) whipping cream

4 oz (114 g) bittersweet chocolate

1 Combine crumbs and butter. Press firmly on bottom of 8 1/2 " (22 cm) springform pan.

2 In mixer bowl, beat cream cheese until fluffy. Gradually beat in Eagle Brand and eggs until smooth. Remove half the batter to another bowl; stir in white chocolate and liqueur. To remaining batter, stir in semi-sweet chocolate.

3 Pour the semi-sweet chocolate batter over the prepared crust. Spoon the white chocolate batter over the semi-sweet chocolate layer. Bake at 300°F (150°C) for 45-50 min. Cool.

4 Heat whipping cream. Add bittersweet chocolate and stir until melted. Spoon over cooled cake. Spread to cover top and sides. Top with chocolate curls or garnish as desired. Chill.

TIP:

To make chocolate curls, use a vegetable peeler or thin, sharp knife, slice across a block of room temperature sweet milk chocolate or large-size milk chocolate candy bar with long, thin strokes.

Maple Pumpkin Cheesecake

1/4 cup (50 mL) butter, melted
1 1/4 cups (300 mL) graham cracker crumbs
1/4 cup (50 mL) sugar
3 pkgs (250 g each) cream cheese, softened
1 can (300 mL) **Regular or Low Fat Eagle Brand**®
1/4 cup (50 mL) pure maple syrup
1 can (398 mL) pumpkin
3 eggs
1 1/2 tsp (7.5 mL) ground cinnamon
1 tsp (5 mL) ground nutmeg
1/2 tsp (2.5 mL) salt

1 Combine butter, crumbs and sugar. Press into 9 " (23 cm) springform pan.

2 In large mixing bowl, beat cheese until fluffy. Gradually beat in Eagle Brand until smooth. Add syrup and remaining ingredients; mix until smooth. Pour into prepared pan.

3 Bake at 300°F (150°C) 1 hour and 15 minutes or until set (centre will be slightly soft). Cool thoroughly and chill 4 hours or overnight. Top with Maple Pecan Glaze.

PREP TIME: 25 minutes
plus baking and chilling time
SERVINGS: 8-10

Maple Pecan Glaze:

3/4 cup (175 mL) maple syrup
1 cup (250 mL) whipping cream
1/2 cup (125 mL) chopped pecans

In saucepan, combine maple syrup and whipping cream, bring to a boil. Boil rapidly 15-20 minutes, stirring occasionally. Cool. Add chopped pecans. (Makes 11/4 cups (300 mL)) Glaze chilled cheesecake.

TIP:

Glazes work well over a plain cheesecake. For **Chocolate Glaze**, melt together 4 oz (114 g) bitter-sweet or semi-sweet chocolate with 1/2 cup (125 mL) whipping cream until smooth. Spoon warm over cooled cheesecake. For **Apple Cinnamon**, combine in a small saucepan 1/3 cup (75 mL) frozen apple juice concentrate, thawed, with 1 tsp (5 mL) cornstarch and 1/4 tsp (1 mL) ground cinnamon, until well mixed. Stir over low heat until thickened and bubbly. Cool slightly and pour gently over cooled dessert.

Cheesecakes, Cakes & other

Classic Chocolate Orange Cheesecake

Classic

Your guests will think you fussed for hours over this contemporary classic dessert with its swirls of chocolate and orange ... let them !

PREP TIME: 15 minutes plus baking and chilling time
SERVINGS: 10-12

1/2 cup (125 mL) graham
  wafer crumbs

3 pkgs (250 g each) regular
  or light cream cheese, softened

1 can (300 mL) **Regular
or Low Fat Eagle Brand®**

4 eggs

4 oz (114 g) semi-sweet
  chocolate, melted

2 tsp (30 mL) orange liqueur
  or juice

1 tsp (5 mL) grated orange rind

1 Sprinkle crumbs over bottom and sides of greased 9″ (23 cm) springform pan.

2 Beat cream cheese until fluffy; gradually add Eagle Brand. Beat in eggs.

3 Measure out 1 1/4 cups (300 mL) cheese mixture; stir in melted chocolate, and set aside.

4 Add orange liqueur and rind to remaining cheese mixture; pour into prepared pan.

5 Drop spoonfuls of chocolate mixture into pan. Swirl through mixtures with knife to marble.

6 Bake in preheated 325°F (160°C) oven for 50-55 minutes or until set. Cool thoroughly and chill 4 hours or overnight.

TIP:

To soften cream cheese quickly, unwrap and place on a microwave-safe plate. Microwave on 50% power (MEDIUM) 1 to 1 1/2 minutes or until cream cheese is soft.

Rum'n Eggnog Cheesecake

1 1/3 cups (325 mL) graham wafer crumbs
1/4 cup (50 mL) butter, melted
3 pkgs (250 g each) cream cheese, softened
1 can (300 mL) **Regular or Low Fat Eagle Brand**®
3 eggs
1/4 cup (50 mL) rum or 1 tbsp (15 mL) rum extract
1 tbsp (15 mL) orange zest
1/4 tsp (1 mL) ground nutmeg, or to taste
1 cup (250 mL) whipping cream, whipped

1 Combine graham crumbs and melted butter.
Press well into 9" (23 cm) springform pan.

2 Beat cream cheese until fluffy; gradually beat in
Eagle Brand, eggs, rum, zest and nutmeg.
Pour over prepared crust.

3 Bake in preheated 325°F (160°C) oven for 45-50
minutes or until centre is just set. Cool and
chill 4 hours or overnight. Before serving, top with
whipped cream and sprinkle with nutmeg.

PREP TIME: 15 minutes
plus baking and chilling time
SERVINGS: 8-10

Piña Colada Cheesecake

1 cup (250 mL) graham cracker crumbs
3/4 cup (175 mL) flaked coconut
2 tbsp (30 mL) firmly packed brown sugar
1/4 cup (50 mL) butter, melted
2 pkgs (250 g each) cream cheese
1 can (300 mL) **Regular or Low Fat Eagle Brand**®
1/4 tsp (1 mL) coconut extract
1 cup (250 mL) drained, crushed pineapple
3 eggs
1 cup (250 mL) sour cream

PREP TIME: 15 minutes
plus baking and chilling time
SERVINGS: 8-10

1 Combine crumbs, coconut, brown sugar and butter.
Press onto bottom and halfway up sides of a 9"
(23 cm) springform pan.

2 Whip cream cheese until fluffy. Add Eagle Brand
and mix until smooth. Add coconut extract and
pineapple, then eggs. Mix well.

3 Pour into prepared pan. Bake in preheated 350°F
(180°C) oven 55-60 minutes or until centre is set.

4 Cool thoroughly and chill 4 hours or overnight.
Remove from springform pan and spread sour
cream on top. Garnish as desired.

Cheesecakes, Cakes & other

Keylime Squares

PREP TIME: 15 minutes plus baking and chilling time
SERVINGS: 9 squares

1 1/4 cups (300 mL) graham
 cracker crumbs
1/4 cup (50 mL) sugar
3 tbsp (45 mL) butter, melted
3 tbsp (45 mL) sugar
2 tbsp (30 mL) cornstarch
1 can (300 mL) **Regular or
 Low Fat Eagle Brand**®
1 large egg
Grated zest of 1 lime
1/2 cup (125 mL) fresh lime juice

1 Mix together crumbs, 1/4 cup (50 mL) sugar,
 and butter until well combined. Press onto bottom
 and up sides of a parchment paper-lined 9 x 9-inch
 (2 L) baking pan. Place in refrigerator or freezer to firm.

2 In medium bowl, combine 3 tbsp (45 mL) sugar
 and cornstarch. Gradually stir in Eagle Brand, then
 the egg. Add the lime zest and lime juice; stir just
 until combined. Take crust from refrigerator
 and immediately pour filling overtop.

3 Bake in preheated 325°F (160°C) oven 25 minutes
 or until the edges look firm, but centre is still slightly
 unset. Cool completely. Cover and chill 2 hours or
 overnight. Cut into bars. Serve chilled with
 whipped cream, berries, or as desired.

TIP:

Keylimes are available from early winter to late summer months. You can also, of course, use regular
limes.

Cranberry Crumb Squares

3/4 cup (175 mL) butter, softened
1/3 cup (75 mL) icing sugar
1 1/2 cups (375 mL) all-purpose flour
1 pkg (250 g) cream cheese, softened
1 can (300 mL) **Regular or Low Fat Eagle Brand**®
1/4 cup (50 mL) lemon juice
3 tbsp (45 mL) brown sugar, divided
2 tbsp (30 mL) corn starch
1 can (398 mL) whole cranberry sauce
1/4 cup (50 mL) cold butter
1/3 cup (1/3 mL) all-purpose flour
3/4 cup (175 mL) chopped walnuts

PREP TIME: 15 minutes
plus baking time
SERVINGS: 8-10

1 Cream together softened butter and icing sugar until light and fluffy. Gradually beat in 1 1/2 cups (375 mL) flour. Press onto bottom of 13 x 9″ (3.5 L) baking pan and bake in preheated 350°F (180°C) oven 15 minutes or until lightly browned. Reduce oven temperature to 325°F (160°C).

2 In large mixer bowl, beat cream cheese until fluffy and gradually beat in Eagle Brand until smooth. Stir in lemon juice. Pour over crust in pan.

3 Combine 1 tbsp (15mL) brown sugar and corn starch; mix well. Blend in cranberry sauce. Spoon evenly over cheese mixture.

4 Combine remaining brown sugar and 1/3 cup (75 mL) flour in medium mixing bowl. Cut in cold butter with pastry blender until crumbly. Stir in nuts. Sprinkle evenly over cranberry mixture.

5 Bake 45 to 50 minutes or until bubbly and golden. Cool. Cut into squares. Serve warm or chilled.

TIP:
For a different flavour profile and to make it 'tipsy', add 1 tbsp (45 mL) cherry-flavoured Kirsch or orange-flavoured Cuantro liqueur to the cranberry sauce mixture.

Cheesecakes, Cakes & other

100 Reasons Anniversary Cake

PREP TIME: 15 minutes plus baking and chilling time
SERVINGS: 10-12 portions

1 pkg (510 g) yellow or white cake mix
1 can (300 mL) **Regular or Low Fat Eagle Brand**®
2 tbsp (30 mL) frozen orange or pineapple juice concentrate, thawed
1 tsp (5 mL) grated orange rind
3-4 cups (750 mL-1 L) whipped cream or vanilla frosting

1 Prepare and bake cake as package directs for 13 x 9″ (3.5 L) pan. Cool cake and leave in pan.

2 Using a table-knife handle, poke holes throughout cake, about 1-inch (2.5 cm) apart and halfway to bottom.

3 Combine Eagle Brand, orange juice concentrate and orange rind; mix well. Spoon small amount of mixture into each cake hole; spread remaining mixture evenly over top. Chill 3-4 hours.

4 Just before serving, spread whipped cream or frosting over cake and garnish as desired.

TIP:

For an extra flavour kick, ice your cake with Eagle Brand's Spiced Frosting, found on p. 115.

Chocolate Tres Leches

PREP TIME: 10 min. plus baking and chilling time
SERVINGS: 8-10

1 pkg (510 g) chocolate or vanilla
cake mix
1 can (300 mL) **Regular or
Low Fat Eagle Brand**®
3/4 cup (175 mL) whipping cream,
unwhipped
3/4 cup (175 mL) coconut milk
or evaporated milk
1/2 tsp (2.5 mL) rum extract
1/2 tsp (2.5 mL) vanilla extract
3 tbsp (45 mL) unsweetened
cocoa powder, sifted
1/4 tsp (1 mL) cinnamon

1 Prepare cake mix as directed, in one 13 x 9 "
(3.5 L) layer.

2 Combine Eagle Brand, cream and coconut milk with
extracts. Remove 1/2 cup (125 mL) mixture to a
small bowl; whisk in cocoa powder and cinnamon
until smooth. Slowly whisk chocolate mixture back
into larger milk mixture.

3 Remove baked cake from oven. Cool slightly and
transfer to a larger baking pan or deep serving dish.
Using a fork, poke holes liberally in top and sides
of cake. While cake is still warm, pour half the milk
mixture overtop. Wait one minute and pour
remainder over cake.

4 Cover and chill 1 hour.

TIP:

Garnish suggestions: white & dark chocolate curls, sprinkled with cinnamon & cocoa; fresh pears
on the side, peeled and thinly sliced; gooseberries or raspberries; fresh pineapple and mango, sprinkled
with toasted coconut.

Dark Chocolate Coconut Cake

PREP TIME: 15 minutes plus baking and chilling time
SERVINGS: 10-12

4 eggs
3/4 cup (75 mL) sugar
2 1/2 cups (625 mL) shredded
  or dessicated coconut
1 cup (250 mL) ground almonds
1/3 cup (75 mL) butter, melted
1 tsp (5 mL) almond extract (optional)
1 can (300 mL) **Regular or
  Low Fat Eagle Brand**®
3/4 cup (125 mL) glacé fruit
  or bing cherries, well-drained
  OR
1/2 cup (125 mL) apricot jelly or
  cherry jam (see step 3)
1 pkg (170 g) dark or semi-sweet
  chocolate, chopped
1/4 cup (50 mL) whipping cream,
  unwhipped

1 In large bowl, beat eggs and sugar until light and creamy. Fold in coconut, almonds, butter, Eagle Brand and fruit.

2 Pour mixture into a 9"x13" (3.5 L) parchment paper-lined baking pan and bake in preheated 350°F (180°C) oven 20-25 minutes or until golden. Cool.

3 If using jelly glaze, spread 1/2 cup (125 mL) apricot jelly or cherry jam over cooled cake base.

4 Over low heat, melt chocolate with cream. Remove from heat and let cool to room temperature. Pour topping over cake. Chill one hour. Remove from pan using paper. Slice and garnish as desired.

Fast 'n' Fabulous Fruitcake Classic

The season would not be the same without this classic holiday offering. Easy to make ahead and freeze for season entertaining and gift-giving, this moist and hearty fruitcake is one of Eagle Brand's top 10 recipes of all time.

PREP TIME: 20 minutes plus baking time
SERVINGS: Each cake serves 8-10

2 1/2 cups (625 mL) all-purpose flour
1 tsp (5 mL) baking soda
2 eggs, slightly beaten
1 jar (750 mL) mincemeat
1 can (300 mL) **Regular or Low Fat Eagle Brand**®
1/4 cup (50 mL) dark rum (optional)
2 cups (500 mL) chopped mixed glacé fruit
1 cup (250 mL) chopped walnuts
Whole glacé cherries

1 Stir together flour and baking soda; set aside.

2 Combine eggs, mincemeat, Eagle Brand, rum (if using), chopped fruit and nuts. Add dry ingredients; mix well.

3 Divide batter between two prepared 9 x 5-inch (1.5 L) loaf pans.

4 Bake in a preheated oven for 1 hour and 20-25 minutes or until done. Cool 15 minutes. Turn out pans; cool completely. Garnish with glacé cherries.

TIP:

For a change of taste and look, substitute the usual glacé fruit mix with a glittering golden combination, in similar amounts, of glacé pineapple, golden raisins and a hint of candied ginger. Use light rum for the 'tipsy' version.

Lemon Refrigerator Squares

A classic no-bake recipe from the 1930's...made for the 'modern' refrigerator.

PREP TIME: 10 minutes
plus chilling time
SERVINGS: 9 squares

1 can (300 mL) Regular or Low Fat Eagle Brand®
1/2 cup (125 mL) lemon juice
1 tsp (5 mL) grated lemon rind
27 graham wafer biscuits
2 cups (500 mL) whipping cream, whipped (optional)

1 Blend Eagle Brand, lemon juice and lemon rind until mixture thickens. Line an 8-inch (20 cm) square pan with parchment paper, then place 9 graham wafer biscuits, fitted together, to cover bottom of pan.

2 Spread with half the lemon filling, making sure biscuits remain in place. Repeat with layer of 9 biscuits and lemon filling. Top with remaining 9 biscuits. Chill 6 hours or until set.

3 Remove dessert from pan and peel off paper. Cut into squares and serve topped with whipped cream.

Morning Apple Cake

PREP TIME: 15 minutes
plus baking time
SERVINGS: 6 to 8

1 can (300 mL) **Regular or Low Fat Eagle Brand**®
2 eggs
1/4 cup (50 mL) butter, melted
3 cups (750 mL) biscuit baking mix
1/2 tsp (2.5 mL) ground cinnamon (or to taste)
2 cups (500 mL) applesauce
1 1/2 cups (375 mL) chopped pecans
1 cup (250 mL) raisins (optional)
2 apples, cored, peeled and thinly sliced

1 Whisk together Eagle Brand, eggs and melted butter. Stir in baking mix, cinnamon, applesauce, pecans and raisins if using.

2 Pour batter evenly into parchment paper-lined 13 x 9 " (3.5 L) baking dish. Arrange the apples in rows over batter.

3 Bake in preheated 325°F (160°C) oven 40 to 45 minutes or until knife inserted in centre comes out clean. Serve warm or at room temperature. Garnish as desired.

TIP:
A tart baking apple such as Granny Smith, Empire or Northern Spy hold their shape during baking and work best for this recipe.

Cheesecakes, Cakes & other

Surprise-in-a Pocket Cupcakes

3 eggs
1 pkg (250 g) cream cheese, softened
1 can (300 mL) **Regular or Low Fat Eagle Brand**®
1 pkg (2-layer size) chocolate cake mix
1 1/3 cups (325 mL) water
Prepared chocolate frosting
Candy sprinkles

1 Separate 1 egg yolk from white. Beat cream cheese until fluffy. Gradually beat in 1/3 cup (75 mL) Eagle Brand and egg yolk; set aside.

2 Combine cake mix, remaining Eagle Brand, water, 2 eggs and egg white. Beat on low speed until moistened; beat on high speed for 2 minutes.

3 Line muffin pans with 30 large paper baking cups. Divide batter among baking cups, filling each about 3/4 full. Add a rounded teaspoonful of the cream cheese mixture to the centre of each.

4 Bake in preheated 350°F (180°C) oven for 20-25 minutes or until tops spring back when lightly touched. (Filling will sink during baking.) Cool on wire racks. Decorate cupcakes with frosting and candy sprinkles.

PREP TIME: 20 minutes plus baking time
SERVINGS: 30 cupcakes

Magic Midget Donuts

Another classic from 1933, when housewives' ingenuity made treats from everyday basics… with the help of Eagle Brand !

1 loaf fresh bread (white, whole wheat, raisin)
1 can (300 mL) **Regular or Low Fat Eagle Brand**®
Oil for frying

1 Spoon Eagle Brand in small amounts onto a plate.

2 Remove crusts from bread, if desired, and cut bread into 1 or 2-inch (2.5 or 5 cm) cubes. Roll in a ball and then roll in Eagle Brand quickly just to coat.

3 Fry in deep fryer set at 360-375° F (185-190°C) one minute or until golden brown. Remove and set on paper towel-lined baking sheets to cool.

PREP TIME: 20 minutes
SERVINGS: 3 dozen

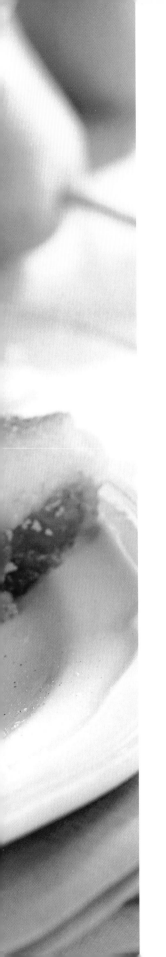

Pies, Tarts & Crumbles

From the first time a pie ever wafted its fresh-baked aroma from a kitchen window sill, this homemade dessert has been the centrepiece of family dinners, picnics and holiday tables. Whether it's pumpkin, apple, blueberry, peach or pear... coconut or pecan... white or dark chocolate... butter, sugar or maple syrup... topped with fruit or stuffed with caramel, creamy Eagle Brand makes this luscious dessert "easy as pie".

So many Eagle Brand pies from the 1920's have become classics, and you'll find them here. Cherry-O-Cheese Pie boasts a no-bake lemony filling which magically thickens without cooking or baking. Perfect Pumpkin Pie is rich, perfectly spiced and only five minutes to prepare. And diner classics creamy Lemon Meringue and tangy cousin Key Lime still top the list of favourites to this day.

Whether it's timeless berry crumble or trendy Banoffee pie, Eagle Brand guarantees chef-quality results for your kitchen window sill!

Magic Lemon Meringue Pie

Classic

Truly the best lemon meringue pie ever, this recipe debuted in the 1940's as "Lemon Ice Box Pie" and quickly became the most popular dessert of that decade. Mmmmmm-magic!

PREP TIME: 15 minutes plus baking time
SERVINGS: 6-8

3 eggs, separated
2 tsp (10 mL) grated lemon rind
1 can (300 mL) **Regular or
   Low Fat Eagle Brand**®
1/2 cup (125 mL) lemon juice
1 (9"/23 cm) baked pastry shell or
   prepared graham pie crust
1/4 tsp (1 mL) cream of tartar
1/4 cup (50 mL) sugar

1 Beat egg yolks; whisk in lemon rind, Eagle Brand and lemon juice. Pour into prepared crust.

2 Bake in preheated 325°F (160°C) oven for 25 minutes. Remove from oven. Increase oven temperature to 350°F (180°C).

3 Beat egg whites with cream of tartar until foamy; gradually add sugar beating until stiff peaks form but not dry. Spread meringue on top of hot pie, sealing carefully to edge of crust.

4 Return to oven and bake for 10 minutes or until meringue is golden brown. Cool. Chill before serving, if desired.

Cool 'n Sassy Keylime Pie

Substitute keylime juice for lemon juice, and add 2-3 drops of green food colouring, if desired. Top with a meringue as above, or with whipped cream.

Irresistible Sugar Pie

Fill your kitchen with the aroma of maple syrup as this traditional Québec favourite bakes in the oven.

1 (9 "/23 cm) unbaked pie shell
2 eggs, beaten
1 can (300 mL) **Regular or Low Fat Eagle Brand**®
1 cup (250 mL) maple syrup
1/2 cup (125 mL) walnut or pecan pieces (optional)

1 Whisk eggs; stir in Eagle Brand and maple syrup until thoroughly combined. Pour into pie shell. Sprinkle nuts over top, if desired..

2 Bake in preheated 425ºF (220ºC) oven for 10 minutes.

3 Reduce heat to 350ºF (180ºC). Continue baking 15 to 20 minutes longer or until set.

PREP TIME: 5 minutes
plus baking time
SERVINGS: 6-8

Caramel Apple Streusel Pie

1/3 cup (75 mL) brown sugar
1/3 cup (75 mL) all-purpose flour
Pinch ground cinnamon
4 tbsp (45 mL) butter
1/3 cup (75 mL) chopped pecans
4 oz (114 g) caramels, unwrapped (about 16)
1 can (300 mL) **Regular or Low Fat Eagle Brand**®
2 apples, cored, peeled and sliced
1/4 cup (50 mL) raisins (optional)
1 (9 "/23 cm) graham cracker ready pie crust

PREP TIME: 15 minutes
plus baking time
SERVINGS: 6-8

1 Combine sugar, flour and cinnamon. Cut in 2 tbsp (30 mL) butter until mixture becomes crumbly. Stir in pecans and set aside.

2 Combine remaining butter with caramels and Eagle Brand over low heat. Cook, stirring constantly until melted and smooth. Stir in apples and raisins, if using and then spoon into pie crust. Top with reserved crumb mixture.

3 Bake in preheated 325°F (160°C) oven for 35 to 40 minutes or until hot and bubbly.

Cherry-O Cheese Pie Classic

Introduced in the 1950s, this unbelievably easy and creamy refrigerator pie can be dressed up for company, or brought to the table for an after dinner treat.

PREP TIME: 10 minutes
plus chilling time
SERVINGS: 6-8

1 pkg (250 g) cream cheese, softened
1 can (300 mL) **Regular or Low Fat Eagle Brand**®
1/3 cup (75 mL) lemon juice
1 tsp (5 mL) vanilla extract
1 (9/23 cm) prepared graham cracker crust or
  baked pastry shell
1 can (19 oz/540 mL) cherry pie filling, chilled
Sliced almonds, grilled (optional)

1 In mixer bowl, beat cheese until fluffy. Gradually add Eagle Brand; blend thoroughly. Stir in lemon juice and vanilla.

2 Pour into prepared crust. Chill 3 hours or until set.

3 Top with desired amount of pie filling before serving. Garnish with grilled almonds, or as desired.

Dutch Peach Pie

PREP TIME: 15 minutes
plus baking time
SERVINGS: 6-8

1 can (796 mL) sliced peaches, well drained
1 (9"/23 cm) homemade or prepared pastry shell
2 eggs, beaten
1 can (300 mL) **Regular or Low Fat Eagle Brand**®
1/4 cup (50 mL) butter, melted
1/2 cup (125 mL) brown sugar
1/2 cup (125 mL) all-purpose flour
1/4 cup (50 mL) cold butter
1/3 cup (75 mL) chopped pecans

1 Arrange peaches in prepared pastry shell.

2 Whisk together eggs, Eagle Brand and butter; pour over peaches.

3 Combine brown sugar and flour. Cut in cold butter until mixture resembles coarse crumbs; stir in nuts. Sprinkle over pie.

4 Bake in preheated 375°F (190°C) oven for 35-40 minutes or until golden brown. Cool. Serve at room temperature or chilled.

Light 'n Luscious Banana Cream Pie

1 large banana
Orange juice
1 (9"/23 cm) baked pie crust
3 tbsp (45 mL) corn starch
1/4 tsp (1 mL) salt
1 2/3 cups (400 mL) water
1 can (300 mL) Regular or Low Fat Eagle Brand®
3 egg yolks
2 tbsp (30 mL) butter
2 tbsp (30 mL) vanilla extract
2 cups (500 mL) frozen light whipped topping,
  thawed

1 Slice banana; dip in orange juice and drain. Arrange slices on bottom of prepared crust.

2 Dissolve cornstarch and salt in water; whisk in Eagle Brand and egg yolks.

3 Cook over a medium heat, whisking constantly until thickened and bubbly. Remove from heat; stir in butter and vanilla.

4 Pour filling over sliced bananas; cool. Cover and chill overnight. Serve with whipped topping and garnish as desired.

PREP TIME: 20 minutes
plus chilling time
SERVINGS: 6-8

Fluffy Lemon Berry Pie

1 can (300 mL) **Regular or Low Fat Eagle Brand**®
3/4 cup (175 mL) frozen lemonade concentrate, thawed
2 cups (500 mL) whipping cream, whipped
1 (9"/23 cm) prepared graham cracker crust or
  baked pastry shell
Fresh seasonal berries

1 Combine Eagle Brand and lemonade concentrate; mix well.

2 Fold in whipped cream. Spoon mixture into prepared crust.

3 Chill 4 hours or until set. Top with fruit of choice.

PREP TIME: 15 minutes
plus chilling time
SERVINGS: 6-8

Perfect Pumpkin Pie *Classic*

One of the first recipes to come out of the Eagle Brand kitchen in 1927, we've improved on tradition with an even easier, silkier and tastier version we can't help but call "perfect".

PREP TIME: 5 minutes
plus baking time
SERVINGS: 6-8

1 can (398 mL) pumpkin
1 can (300 mL) **Regular or Low Fat Eagle Brand**®
2 eggs
2 tbsp (30 mL) brown sugar
1/2 tsp (2.5 mL) each: ground cinnamon, mace and salt
1 (9"/23 cm) unbaked deep dish frozen pastry shell

1 Whisk together pumpkin, Eagle Brand, eggs, brown sugar and spices. Pour into unbaked pastry shell.

2 Bake in preheated 425°F (220°C) oven 15 minutes. Reduce oven temperature to 350°F (180°C). Bake an additional 35 to 40 minutes or until knife inserted near centre comes out clean. Cool. Garnish as desired.

Heavenly Harvest Pumpkin Tarts

PREP TIME: 5 minutes
plus baking time
SERVINGS: 24 tarts

1 can (300 mL) **Regular or Low Fat Eagle Brand**®
1 1/4 cups (300 mL) canned pumpkin
2 tbsp (30 mL) brown sugar
1 egg
1/4 tsp (1 mL) each: ground cinnamon and nutmeg
24 (3"/7.5 cm) unbaked tart shells

1 Whisk together Eagle Brand, pumpkin, brown sugar, egg, cinnamon and nutmeg. Pour evenly into tart shells.

2 Bake in preheated 375°F (190°C) oven for 18 minutes or until centre is just set and pastry is golden. Cool and garnish as desired.

Pies, Tarts & Crumbles

Cranberry Pumpkin Pie

PREP TIME: 15 minutes plus baking time
SERVINGS: 8 to 12

3 cups (750 mL) finely crushed gingersnaps

1/3 cup (75 mL) butter, melted

1 cup (250 mL) frozen or fresh cranberries

1 can (398 mL) pumpkin

1 can (300 mL) **Regular or Low Fat Eagle Brand**®

2 eggs

2 tbsp (30 mL) brown sugar

1/2 tsp (2.5 mL) each: ground cinnamon, mace and salt

1/2 cup (125 mL) coarsely crushed gingersnaps

1/2 cup (125 mL) dried cranberries

1 Combine cookie crumbs with butter; pat onto bottom and up sides of deep dish 9 " (23 cm) pie plate. Bake in a preheated 425°F (220°C) oven for 8 minutes or until lightly toasted. Let cool slightly.

2 Sprinkle frozen or fresh cranberries over bottom.

3 Whisk together pumpkin, Eagle Brand, eggs, brown sugar and spices. Pour over cranberries.

4 In small bowl, mix together coarsely crushed gingersnaps and dried cranberries; sprinkle evenly over pumpkin filling.

5 Bake 15 minutes at 425°F (220°C). Reduce oven temperature to 350°F (180°C) and bake an additional 35 to 40 minutes or until knife inserted near centre comes out clean. Cool completely.

Beg for More Crumble

PREP TIME: 15 min. plus baking time
SERVINGS: 6

1 can (300 mL) **Regular or Low Fat Eagle Brand**®
1/4 cup (50 mL) orange juice
1/2 tsp (2.5 mL) each: ground cinnamon and nutmeg
3 apples peeled, cored and sliced
3 pears, peeled, cored and sliced
1/2 cup (125 mL) frozen cranberries, thawed
1 cup (250 mL) all-purpose flour
1/2 cup (125 mL) rolled oats
1/2 cup (125 mL) brown sugar
1/2 cup (125 mL) cold butter

1 Whisk together Eagle Brand, orange juice, and spices. Add apples, pears and cranberries; toss until fruit is well coated.

2 Spoon mixture into a lightly buttered 8 cup (2 L) baking dish; set aside.

3 Combine flour, oats and sugar. Cut in butter until mixture resembles coarse crumbs; sprinkle on top of apple mixture.

4 Bake in preheated 375°F (190°C) oven for 30-35 minutes or until fruit has softened. Serve warm with ice cream.

Perfect Pecan Pie

1 egg
1 can (300 mL) **Regular or Low Fat Eagle Brand**®
1 cup (250 mL) dark corn syrup
1/4 tsp (1 mL) maple extract
1 (9"/23 cm) frozen pastry shell, unbaked
1 cup (250 mL) pecan halves

1 Beat egg until frothy; thoroughly blend in Eagle Brand, corn syrup and maple extract.

2 Pour filling into unbaked pie shell. Top with pecans.

3 Bake in preheated 425°F (220°C) oven 10 minutes; reduce heat to 350°F (180°C) and bake 25 minutes longer or until centre is softly set. Do not overbake. Cool before cutting.

PREP TIME: 10 minutes plus baking time
SERVINGS: 6-8

Sweet 'n Spicy Baked Apples

These nutmeg-spiced baked apples are the perfect ending to a fall meal, and a great way to warm your insides in the chilly fall air.

6 medium baking apples (about 2 lbs) such as Northern Spy, Cortland or Golden Delicious
1/3 cup (75 mL) mixed dried fruit bits or raisins
1 can (300 mL) **Regular or Low Fat Eagle Brand**®
1 tbsp (15 mL) water
1/4 tsp (1 mL) ground nutmeg

1 Core apples; peel a strip from the top of each. If necessary cut thin slice from bottom of each apple so apple will stand upright. Place apples upright in greased 11x7-inch (2 L) baking dish. Fill centres with fruit bits, trail mix or raisins.

2 Combine Eagle Brand, water and nutmeg; pour over and around apples.

3 Set dish in a 13x9-inch (3 L) ovenproof pan; set on oven rack. Carefully pour boiling water into outer pan to a 1-inch (2.5 cm) depth. Bake in preheated 350°F (180°C) oven 40 to 45 minutes or until apples are tender, occasionally spooning Eagle Brand mixture in bottom of dish over apples. Serve warm.

PREP TIME: 10 minutes plus baking time
SERVINGS: 6

Banoffee Pie

PREP TIME: 20 minutes
plus chilling time
SERVINGS: 6-8

3 bananas, peeled and sliced
1 (9"/23 cm) prepared graham crumb crust or baked pie shell
1 can (300 mL) **Regular or Low Fat Eagle Brand**®
2 tsp (10 mL) instant coffee
2 tsp (10 mL) warm water
2-3 cups (500-750 mL) frozen whipped topping, thawed

1 Place bananas over bottom of prepared crust.

2 Caramelize Eagle Brand (see p.128). Stir until smooth and cool slightly. Spoon caramelized milk over bananas.

3 Stir together coffee and water until well combined. Gently stir into whipped topping; spoon over caramelized milk. Chill 2 hours.

Chocolate Truffle Pie

PREP TIME: 10 minutes
plus chilling time
SERVINGS: 6-8

1 envelope (7 g) unflavoured gelatine
1/2 cup (125 mL) water
3 squares (28 g each) unsweetened or semi-sweet chocolate, melted and cooled
1 can (300 mL) **Regular or Low Fat Eagle Brand**®
1 tsp (5 mL) vanilla extract
2 cups (500 mL) whipping cream, whipped
1 (9"/23 cm) prepared chocolate crumb crust

1 In small saucepan, sprinkle gelatine over water; let stand 1 minute. Over low heat, stir until gelatine dissolves. Cool.

2 Beat melted, cooled chocolate with Eagle Brand. Stir in gelatine mixture and vanilla. Fold in whipped cream.

3 Pour into prepared crust. Chill 2 hours or until set. Garnish as desired.

TIP:

For an easy gluten-free crust for no-bake pies, combine 2 cups of toasted flaked coconut with 1/3 cup of melted butter and chill 20 minutes to set.

Okanagan Pear Tart

PREP TIME: 15 minutes plus baking & chilling time
SERVINGS: 8

2 cups (500 mL) digestive biscuits, finely crushed (1/2 of 400g package)
1/3 cup (75 mL) butter, melted
1/4 cup (50 mL) apricot jam
1 can (796 mL) pear halves, well drained
1 can (300 mL) **Regular or Low Fat Eagle Brand**®
1 egg
1/4 cup (50 mL) whipping cream, unwhipped
1/2 tsp (2.5 mL) vanilla extract
Pinch cinnamon

1 Mix biscuit crumbs with butter until well moistened. Spread mixture onto bottom and sides of a 9-inch (23 cm) tart pan or pie dish. Refrigerate 10 minutes.

2 Spread jam over chilled crust. Arrange pear halves over jam layer to cover surface completely.

3 Whisk together Eagle Brand, egg, whipping cream, vanilla and cinnamon; pour over pears.

4 Place tart pan on baking sheet. Bake in preheated 375°F (190°C) oven 50 minutes or until top is golden and just set. Cool in pan. Garnish as desired.

TIP:

If using fresh pears, slice and boil 4 pears in 3 cups (750 mL) water and 4 tbsp (60 mL) sugar, until tender.

Holiday Chocolate Stout Pie

PREP TIME: 20 minutes plus baking and chilling time
SERVINGS: two-9" tarts, 16 servings each

2 cups (500 mL) graham cracker crumbs
1/2 cup (125 mL) butter, melted
2 tsp (10 mL) grated orange rind
1 can (300 mL) **Regular or Low Fat Eagle Brand**®
1 cup (250 mL) dark stout beer
1 tbsp (15 mL) pure vanilla extract
1 1/2 lbs (750 g) bittersweet chocolate, finely chopped
2 1/4 cups (550 mL) mini-marshmallows
2 cups (500 mL) shelled pistachio nuts and/or toasted slivered almonds
2 cups (500 mL) dried cranberries or lingonberries

1 Combine graham crumbs, butter and orange rind; press onto bottom of parchment-paper lined 13 x 9" (3.5 L) baking pan or two ungreased 9"/23 cm tart pans with removabe bottoms. Bake in centre of preheated 350°F (180°C) oven for 10 minutes. Let cool.

2 In large bowl, combine chocolate and marshmallows; set aside. In saucepan, combine Eagle Brand, beer and vanilla; bring just to a boil. Pour over chocolate and marshmallows; whisk until both are completely melted and mixture is smooth. Fold in nuts and fruit of choice.

3 Spread mixture evenly over prepared crust. Cover and refrigerate for 12 hours. Slice while still cold. Let sit 20 minutes at room temperature before serving.

Can be frozen, wrapped in plastic wrap and overwrapped in foil, for up to 1 month.

Thanks to Culinary Team Canada 2004 for this gold medal winning gourmet dessert … ready in record time !

Chocadamia Delight

PREP TIME: 15 minutes plus baking time
SERVINGS: 8-10

2 cups (500 mL) finely crushed
shortbread cookies
6-7 tbsp (90-105 mL) butter, melted
4 oz (114 g) macadamia nuts,
cut in half
1 pkg (250 g) cream cheese,
softened
1 can (300 mL) **Regular or
Low Fat Eagle Brand**®
1 pkg (225 g) white chocolate
chips, melted
1 egg
1 square (1 oz/28 g) melted dark
chocolate

1 Combine cookie crumbs with butter; pat into
11 "(28 cm) tart pan with removable bottom.
Sprinkle bottom of crust with half of the nuts.

2 Beat cream cheese until fluffy. Gradually beat in
Eagle Brand, white chocolate and egg. Pour into pan
and sprinkle remaining nuts over top.

3 Bake in preheated 375°F (190°C) oven for
25-30 minutes or just until set. Cool. Chill, if
desired.

4 Drizzle dark chocolate over top.

Divine Date Tart

PREP TIME: 20 minutes
plus baking and chilling time
SERVINGS: 6-8

2 cups (500 mL) finely crushed digestive biscuits
1/3 cup (75 mL) butter, melted
1 cup (250 mL) seedless dates
1/2 cup (125 mL) blanched almonds
1 can (300 mL) **Regular or Low Fat Eagle Brand®**
1/4 cup (50 mL) whipping cream
1 egg
1 tsp (5 mL) orange blossom water (or 1/4 tsp orange extract)
1/2 tsp (2.5 mL) cinnamon

1 Combine crushed biscuits and butter. Spread on base and up sides of a 9" (23 cm) tart pan. Refrigerate 10 minutes.

2 Finely chop dates with almonds. Add Eagle Brand, cream and egg; mix until smooth. Add orange blossom water and cinnamon; mix well.

3 Pour mixture over biscuit crust and bake in a preheated 400°F (200°C) oven 20-25 minutes or until firm. Cool.

Butter me up Tarts

PREP TIME: 10 minutes
plus baking time
SERVINGS: 24 tarts

24 (3"/7.5 cm) frozen prepared tart shells, thawed
1 can (300 mL) **Regular or Low Fat Eagle Brand®**
1/2 cup (125 mL) brown sugar
1/3 cup (75 mL) corn syrup
2 tbsp (30 mL) butter, softened
1 egg
Pinch cinnamon (optional)
1/3 cup (75 mL) raisins (optional)

1 Whisk together Eagle Brand, brown sugar, corn syrup, butter, egg, cinnamon and raisins, if using. Pour evenly into tart shells.

2 Bake in preheated 375°F (190°C) oven for 18 minutes or until centre is just set and pastry is golden. Serve warm or at room temperature.

TIP:
For plump, soft textured raisins bring a little water to a boil. Turn off the heat. Stir in raisins. Let stand 3-4 minutes. Drain and pat dry.

Pies, Tarts & Crumbles

Sunny Lemon Blueberry Tarts

PREP TIME: 20 minutes plus chilling and baking time
SERVINGS: 4 dozen tarts

1 cup (250 mL) butter, softened
3/4 pkg (170 g) cream cheese, softened
2 cups (500 mL) unsifted flour
1 can (300 mL) **Regular or Low Fat Eagle Brand**®
1 egg, beaten
2 tbsp (30 mL) lemon juice
1 tbsp (15 mL) grated lemon rind
1 1/4 cup (300 mL) fresh or frozen wild blueberries
Icing sugar (optional)

1 Beat butter and cream cheese until fluffy; stir in flour. Cover; chill 1 hour.

2 Divide dough into quarters. On floured surface, shape each quarter into a smooth ball. Divide first quarter into 12 balls. Press onto bottom and up sides of 1 3/4 inch muffin cups. Repeat with remaining dough.

3 Combine Eagle Brand, egg and lemon juice; mix well. Stir in rind. Sprinkle blueberries into prepared cups; fill with Eagle Brand mixture.

4 Bake in preheated 375°F (190°C) oven 20 minutes. Cool in pans; remove. Sprinkle with confectioners sugar, if desired.

Frozen Mixed Berry Pie

PREP TIME: 15 minutes plus freezing time
SERVINGS: 6-8

1 can (300 mL) **Regular or Low Fat Eagle Brand**®
1/2 cup (125 mL) lemon juice
1 1/2-2 cups (375-500 mL) assorted fresh berries (raspberries, blueberries, blackberries, etc.)
1 container (1 L) frozen whipped topping, thawed
1 (9 "/23 cm) prepared graham cracker or chocolate flavoured crumb crust
Extra berries for garnish, if desired.

1 Stir together Eagle Brand and lemon juice until well combined. Mix in berries.

2 Fold in whipped topping.

3 Spoon mixture into prepared crust. Freeze 5 hours or until set. Let stand 30-40 minutes before serving. Garnish as desired.

TIP:

Plan to take frozen cakes or pies out of the freezer 10 minutes before serving. This will "take the chill off" so your knife will easily glide right through the dessert.

Frozen Peanut Butter Pie

PREP TIME: 20 minutes plus freezing time
SERVINGS: 6-8

1 (9 "/23 cm) Chocolate Crunch Crust*
  or ready-made chocolate crumb crust
1 pkg (250 g) cream cheese, softened
1 can (300 mL) **Regular or
  Low Fat Eagle Brand**®
3/4 cup (175 mL) smooth peanut
  butter
2 tbsp (30 mL) lemon juice
1 tsp (5 mL) vanilla extract
1 cup (250 mL) whipping cream,
  whipped
Chocolate fudge ice cream topping

1 In large mixer bowl, beat cheese until fluffy; gradually beat in Eagle Brand then peanut butter until smooth.

2 Stir in lemon juice and vanilla. Fold in whipped cream.

3 Pour into prepared crust. Drizzle topping over pie. Freeze 4 hours or until firm.

TIP:

*Chocolate Crunch Crust: In heavy saucepan, over low heat, melt 1/3 cup (75 mL) butter and 1 pkg (175 g) semi-sweet chocolate chips. Remove from heat; gently stir in 2 cups (625 mL) toasted rice cereal until completely coated. Press onto bottom and up sides of buttered 9 " (23 cm) pie plate. Chill 30 minutes.

Mousses, Puddings & Trifles

Nobody makes comfort food like Eagle Brand. Since bakers discovered the magic they could produce with Eagle Brand and simple ingredients like chocolate, lemon, or eggs, a world of creativity opened up – and, continues to unfold to this day. Elaborate-looking desserts come together quickly and effortlessly– some even unbaked, with the magic of Eagle Brand.

Old family favourites like custards and puddings have evolved over the decades into luscious layered trifles, mousses and parfaits. And hearty homemade rice and bread puddings in flavours like chocolate, maple rum, cranberry hazelnut, spiced apple and sweet orange, have become not only delightful endings for a Sunday dinner, but favourite treats for holiday times and homecomings.

Eagle Brand does it all - from traditional puddings to fun-for-the-kids chocolate Mud Cups, to sophisticated Crème Caramel, Trifles and Tiramisu, sweet and dreamy Eagle Brand has a dessert for all seasons.

Mosaic Mousse

PREP TIME: 20 minutes plus chilling time
SERVINGS: 6-8

2 tsp (10 mL) gelatine
9 squares (250 g) white chocolate, chopped
1 can (300 mL) **Regular or Low Fat Eagle Brand**®
1 tsp (5 mL) vanilla, orange, mint or almond extract
1 1/2 cups (375 mL) whipping cream, whipped
3/4 cup (175 mL) coarsely chopped chocolate wafers
1/2 cup (125 mL) semi-sweet chocolate chips
1/2 cup (125 mL) milk chocolate chips

1 In small bowl, sprinkle gelatine over 3 tbsp (45 mL) cold water. Place bowl in larger pan filled with hot water until gelatine liquefies.

2 Melt white chocolate with Eagle Brand over low heat, stirring until smooth; remove from heat. Whisk gelatine mixture into chocolate mixture; stir in vanilla. Let cool 10 minutes.

3 Fold whipped cream into chocolate mixture 1/3 at a time.

4 Pour one-half of mixture into a 2L trifle or flat bottom glass bowl. Sprinkle crushed cookies over surface. Top with remaining mousse.

5 To make mosaic topping, melt dark and milk chocolate separately on stovetop or in microwave. Pour each evenly over a parchment paper-lined cookie sheet, spreading evenly and thinly. Refrigerate 10 minutes or until firm. Invert cooled chocolate onto cutting surface; cut into mosaic shapes. Arrange over top mousse. Cover bowl and refrigerate 4-6 hours, or for up to 2 days.

Strawberries 'n Cream

PREP TIME: 15 minutes plus chilling time
SERVINGS: 6-8

1 can (300 mL) **Regular or Low Fat Eagle Brand®**
1 1/2 cups (375 mL) cold water
1 pkg (102 g/4 serving size) vanilla instant pudding mix
2 cups (500 mL) whipping cream, whipped
1 pkg (298 g) frozen pound cake, thawed and cubed
4 cups (1 L) fresh strawberries, cleaned, hulled and sliced
1/2 cup (125 mL) strawberry jam
Additional strawberries for garnish
Toasted slivered almonds

1 In large mixer bowl, combine Eagle Brand and water. Add pudding mix; beat well. Chill until thickened, about 20 minutes. Fold in whipped cream.

2 Spoon 2 cups (500 mL) of the pudding mixture into a 4-quart (4 L) round glass serving bowl; top with half of the cake cubes, half the strawberries, half the jam and half the remaining pudding mixture.

3 Repeat step 3, ending with pudding mixture. Chill at least 4 hours.

4 Garnish with additional strawberries and almonds.

TIP:
Although frozen fruit is perfect for purees and sauces and works well in cheesecakes and frozen desserts, we recommend to use only fresh fruit in trifles. Frozen fruit has a much softer texture than fresh fruit and its colour tends to bleed into other ingredients.

Mousses, Pudding & Trifles

Berry Easy Lemon Mousse

PREP TIME: 15 minutes
plus chilling time
SERVINGS: 6 to 8

1 can (300 mL) **Regular or Low Fat Eagle Brand**®
1 tsp (5 mL) finely grated lemon rind
1/3 cup (75 mL) lemon juice
1 cup (250 mL) light vanilla or plain yogurt
2 cups (500 mL) light frozen whipped topping,
   thawed, divided
2/3 cup (150 mL) fresh blueberries or blackberries
2/3 cup (150 mL) fresh raspberries

1 Mix together Eagle Brand, lemon rind and lemon
juice until smooth.

2 Stir in yogurt; fold in 1 1/2 cups (375 mL) whipped
topping.

3 Fill individual parfait or dessert dishes with 1/2 cup
of mixture. Chill 3-4 hours.

4 Just before serving, top with berries and remaining
whipped topping.

TIP:

Eagle Brand thickens "magically" when its pre-cooked blend of milk and sugar is combined with an acid
such as lemon, orange or chocolate. The acid in these ingredients reacts with the Eagle Brand to create
creamy no-bake puddings, pie fillings, frozen desserts, and sauces.

Berries and Marshmallow Cream

PREP TIME: 15 minutes
plus chilling time
SERVINGS: 8

1 can (300 mL) **Regular or Low Fat Eagle Brand**®
2 cups (500 mL) whipping cream
1 tsp (5 mL) vanilla
2 tbsp (30 mL) gelatine
1 cup (250 mL) mini marshmallows
2 cups (500 mL) mixed berries
1/2 cup (125 mL) blackberry jam

1 In medium bowl, beat Eagle Brand, whipping cream
and vanilla until thick and creamy.

2 Meanwhile, dissolve gelatine powder in 3 tbsp (45 mL)
hot water, stirring until completely dissolved. Gradually
whisk gelatine mixture into Eagle Brand mixture.

3 Fold in marshmallows and berries. Spoon into 8
individual serving glasses. Garnish with a dollop of jam
and additional berries. Chill 1 hour or for up to 2 days.

Mousses, Pudding & Trifles

Crème de la Crème Caramel

Learn the secrets of the great chefs with this Eagle Brand recipe for classic Crème Caramel.

PREP TIME: 15 minutes plus baking & chilling time
SERVINGS: 6-8

1/2 cup (125 mL) sugar
4 eggs
1 3/4 cups (425 mL) water
1 can (300 mL) **Regular Eagle Brand**®
1/2 tsp (2.5 mL) vanilla extract
Pinch salt

1 In heavy frypan over medium heat, cook sugar, stirring constantly until melted and caramel-coloured. Pour into 4-cup (1 L) round shallow baking dish, immediately tilting to coat bottom of dish completely.

2 In medium bowl, beat eggs; stir in water, Eagle Brand, vanilla and salt. Pour through a fine sieve into prepared dish.

3 Set dish in larger pan (eg. broiler pan). Fill pan with hot water to a depth of 1 inch (2.5 cm). Bake in preheated 300ºF (150ºC) oven for 40 to 45 minutes or until knife inserted near centre comes out clean.

4 Remove dish from water bath. Cool. Chill. To serve, loosen side of custard with knife; invert onto serving dish with rim; cut into wedges.

TIP:

A bain-marie is a technique used in cooking to heat materials gradually and evenly to a fixed temperature. A smaller container, with the item to be heated (pudding, baked fruit, even cheesecake), is partially immersed in a larger container, with water which is heated to the boiling point.

Easy & Elegant Tiramisu

PREP TIME: 20 minutes plus chilling time
SERVINGS: 10-12

2 pkgs (250 g each) regular or light cream cheese, softened
1 can (300 mL) **Regular or Low Fat Eagle Brand**®
4 tsp (20 mL) rum extract
1 container (1 L) frozen whipped topping, thawed
48 (3-inch/7.5 cm) soft ladyfingers
2/3 cup (150 mL) cold strong coffee
3 oz (85 g) semi-sweet chocolate, grated

1 Beat cream cheese until fluffy; gradually add Eagle Brand and rum extract.

2 Fold in whipped topping; set aside.

3 Line bottom of 12 cup (3 L) serving bowl with 1/4 ladyfingers; brush with 1/4 coffee. Spoon 1/4 Eagle Brand mixture over ladyfingers; sprinkle with 1/4 grated chocolate. Repeat above process three times, ending with layer of grated chocolate.

4 Cover and chill 4 hours or overnight. Garnish as desired.

TIP:

In traditional Italian Tiramisu, mascarpone cheese is used. Milky-white, it has the texture of spreadable thick cream. Sometimes hard to find, and quite expensive, we've duplicated its sweet, creamy texture with Eagle Brand and whipped cream cheese readily available at your grocer.

Chocolate Orange Crème Caramel

PREP TIME: 15 minutes plus baking and chilling time
SERVINGS: 8

1/2 cup (125 mL) sugar
4 eggs
1 can (300 mL) **Regular Eagle Brand®**
3 tbsp (45 mL) unsweetened cocoa
  powder
1 cup (250 mL) water
3/4 cup (175 mL) orange juice
Pinch salt

1 In a heavy frying pan over medium heat, cook sugar, stirring constantly, until melted and caramel-coloured. Pour into a 4-cup (1 L) shallow round baking dish, immediately tilting to coat bottom of dish completely.

2 In a medium bowl, beat eggs with Eagle Brand. In a small bowl, whisk together cocoa powder and 1/4 cup (50 mL) of water until smooth; stir into Eagle brand mixture. Whisk in remaining water, orange juice and salt. Pour through a fine mesh sieve into the prepared baking dish.

3 Set dish in larger pan (i.e. roasting pan), filled with hot water to a depth of 1-inch (2.5 cm). Bake in a preheated 300°F (150°C) oven 45-55 minutes or until knife inserted near centre comes out clean.

4 Remove dish from water bath. Cool; chill. To serve, loosen the side of custard with a knife; invert onto a rimmed serving plate; cut into wedges.

TIP:
Use eight 1/2-cup (125 mL) ramekins for individual servings.

Date Caramel Bread Pudding

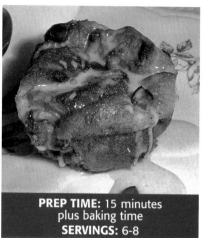

PREP TIME: 15 minutes
plus baking time
SERVINGS: 6-8

1 can (300 mL) **Regular or Low Fat Eagle Brand**®
4 eggs
2/3 cup (150 mL) brown sugar
1 1/2 tsp (7.5 mL) vanilla extract
2-3 tbsp (30-45 mL) rum (optional)
1 1/2 cups (375 mL) water
6 cups (1.5 L) cubed day-old white or French bread
(crusts removed)
1 cup (250 mL) chopped dried dates

1 Whisk together Eagle Brand, eggs, brown sugar, vanilla, rum and water. Stir in bread cubes and dates. Let stand 10 minutes.

2 Spoon mixture into lightly greased 6 cup (1.5 L) baking dish, or 6 large muffin cups.

3 Bake in preheated 350°F (180°C) oven for 45 minutes or until knife inserted in centre comes out clean. Serve warm topped with spiced cream*, if desired.

Blueberry Spice Bread Pudding

PREP TIME: 15 minutes
plus baking time
SERVINGS: 6-8

3 cups (750 mL) day old white or French bread cubes
2 cups (500 mL) fresh or frozen blueberries, rinsed
and drained
3 eggs, beaten
1/2 tsp (2.5 mL) ground cinnamon
1/2 tsp (2.5 mL) ground nutmeg
1 1/2 cups (375 mL) warm water
1 can (300 mL) **Regular or Low Fat Eagle Brand**®
1/4 cup (50 mL) butter, melted
1 tsp (5 mL) vanilla extract

1 Place bread cubes and blueberries in buttered 9" x 9" (2.5 L) baking pan. Mix well.

2 In large bowl, mix together remaining ingredients. Pour evenly over bread cubes and blueberries. Let stand 10 minutes.

3 Bake in preheated 350°F (180°C) oven 45 to 50 minutes or until knife inserted in centre comes out clean. Cool. Serve warm with devon or spiced cream.

TIP:

*Spiced Cream: Add 2 tbsp (30 mL) granulated sugar, and a pinch each of ground cinnamon and nutmeg to 2 cups (500 mL) whipping cream, unwhipped; beat for 3-4 minutes or until mixture thickens and stiff peaks form.

Mousses, Pudding & Trifles

Holiday Bread Pudding Loaf

PREP TIME: 15 minutes plus baking time
SERVINGS: 6-8

1 1/2 cups (375 mL) water
1 cup (250 mL) dried cranberries
5 eggs
1 can (300 mL) **Regular or Low Fat Eagle Brand®**
1 tsp (5 mL) orange zest, or to taste
1/4 cup (50 mL) orange liqueur
1 pinch ground nutmeg, or to taste
1 cup (250 mL) semi-sweet chocolate chips
1 loaf (9.5"/24 cm) day-old egg bread, crusts removed and cut into cubes

1 Bring water just to boil. Remove from heat and stir in cranberries. Let stand 5 to 6 minutes.

2 Whisk together eggs, Eagle Brand, orange zest, liqueur and nutmeg. Stir in chocolate chips and cranberry-water mixture. Stir bread into Eagle Brand mixture and let stand 15 minutes.

3 Spoon mixture into a lightly greased 9 x 5-inch loaf pan. Bake in preheated 325°F (160°C) oven 50 to 55 minutes or until knife inserted in centre comes out clean. Cool and garnish as desired.

TIP:
Always check your baking about 10 minutes before the baking time is up. If the top of your bread pudding is browning too quickly, cover with a sheet of parchment paper, cut to fit the pan

Apple Cinnamon Rice Pudding

PREP TIME: 30 minutes
SERVINGS: 8

3 tbsp (45 mL) butter
1 large apple, peeled, cored & chopped
1 cup (250 mL) uncooked short grain rice
1/3 cup (75 mL) raisins
2 cups (500 mL) unsweetened apple juice
1 tsp (5 mL) ground cinnamon
1/2 tsp (2.5 mL) salt
1/2 tsp (2.5 mL) nutmeg
1 can (300 mL) **Regular or Low Fat Eagle Brand**®

1 In medium saucepan, melt butter; add chopped apple and cook 2 minutes, stirring constantly. Add rice and cook while stirring, for 1 minute.

2 Add raisins and 1/2 cup (125 mL) apple juice; continue stirring for about 1 minute. Add the rest of the apple juice, cinnamon, salt and nutmeg; bring to a boil, stirring occasionally. Cover and cook 15-20 minutes or until rice is tender.

3 Add Eagle Brand; mix well. Reduce heat to medium and continue stirring until smooth and warmed.

4 Cool slightly (pudding thickens as it cools). Serve warm, sprinkled with additional cinnamon, if desired.

Eagle Brand Prune Pudding

Sweet 'n simple. The way mom used to make it.

PREP TIME: 5 minutes
plus baking time
SERVINGS: 6

2 1/2 cups (625 mL) stewed prunes, pitted and chopped
1 can (300 mL) **Regular or Low Fat Eagle Brand**®
Pinch salt
1/4 tsp (1 mL) cinnamon (optional)

1 In a blender container, blend prunes with Eagle Brand and spices. Pour into a lightly greased 8x8" (2 L) baking dish.

2 Bake in preheated 325°F (150°C) oven 40 minutes. Serve with " Lemon Crème" sauce. (See p. 114)

Cranberry Hazelnut Holiday Rice Pudding

PREP TIME: 15 minutes plus cooking time
SERVINGS: 6-8

2 tbsp (30 mL) butter
1/2 cup (125 mL) hazelnuts, chopped
1 cup (250 mL) uncooked short grain rice
1/2 cup (125 mL) dried cranberries
2 tsp (10 mL) finely grated orange rind
1/2 tsp (2 mL) salt
2 cups (500 mL) milk
1 can (300 mL) **Regular or Low Fat Eagle Brand®**

1 In medium saucepan, melt half the butter. Add nuts and cook 5 minutes, stirring often, until nuts are golden brown. Remove to small bowl.

2 Melt remaining butter. Add rice, cranberries, orange rind and salt. Cook, stirring, for 1 minute. Add milk; bring to a boil, stirring occasionally. Reduce heat, cover and simmer for 20 to 25 minutes or until rice is tender.

3 Add Eagle Brand; mix well. Remove from heat and stir in toasted hazelnuts. Serve warm, with cream, if desired.

TIP:
In general, short or medium-grain rices work best for rice puddings, since the starch in them breaks down, helping to thicken the pudding. If you do use long grain rice, make sure you cook it enough. Basmati and wild rice make interesting textural and flavour differences.

Soft Egg Custard

A thin, delicate custard, this Eagle Brand classic is one of the earliest of childhood delights.

PREP TIME: 20 minutes
plus chilling time
SERVINGS: 4 (1/2-cup/125 mL)

1/2 can* (150 mL) **Regular or Low Fat Eagle Brand**®
1 1/2 cups (375 mL) hot water
1/4 tsp (1 mL) salt
3 eggs, slightly beaten
1 tsp (5 mL) vanilla extract

1 Combine Eagle Brand, water and salt in top of double boiler; gradually stir in eggs.

2 Cook over simmering water, stirring constantly, until mixture coats a spoon, about 20 minutes.

3 Remove from heat at once. Cool quickly in a pan of cold water.

4 Stir in vanilla. Pour into four dessert dishes. Chill.

TIP:

*Use leftover Eagle Brand in coffee, tea, hot chocolate or caramelized (see p128) to make a caramel topping sauce for ice cream or cake.

Stained Glass Pudding

PREP TIME: 10 minutes
plus chilling time
SERVINGS: 8 to 10

1 can (300 mL) **Regular or Low Fat Eagle Brand**®
2 1/2 cups (625 mL) cold water
2 pkgs (4-serving size) instant pudding mix, any flavour
1 cup (250 mL) whipping cream, whipped*
3 pkgs (4x99 g ea) commercially prepared jello cups (various colours)

1 Combine Eagle Brand and water. Add pudding mix, beat well. Fold in whipped cream.

2 Cut jello into squares or shapes. In individual glass bowls, arrange pudding and jello squares in alternate layers, making sure jello squares show through the top layer. Chill 1 hour.

*or 1 (4-oz/114 g) container frozen non-dairy whipped topping, thawed.

Mud Cups

1 can (300 mL) **Regular or Low Fat Eagle Brand**®
3/4 cup (175 mL) cold water
1 pkg (4 serving size) instant chocolate pudding mix
2 cups (500 mL) frozen whipped topping, thawed
2/3 cup (150 mL) chocolate cookie crumbs, or to taste
Assorted candies (gummy worms, jelly beans,
   licorice, mini chocolate chips)

1 Combine Eagle Brand and water. Add pudding mix;
  beat until well combined, about 2-3 minutes.

2 Let stand until just thickened, about 12-15 minutes.
  Fold in whipped topping.

3 Spoon Eagle Brand mixture evenly into 8-10
  small-sized cups or bowls. Top each with chocolate
  cookie crumbs. Decorate with gummy worms and
  candies as desired cups, bowls or small clean
  planters lined with plastic wrap.

PREP TIME: 15 minutes
SERVINGS: 8-10

Creamy Banana Pudding

1 can (300 mL) **Regular or Low Fat Eagle Brand**®
1 1/2 cups (375 mL) cold water
1 pkg (4 serving size) vanilla instant pudding mix
2 cups (500 mL) whipping cream, whipped
36 vanilla wafers
3 bananas, sliced, dipped in lemon juice, well drained

1 In a large mixer bowl, combine Eagle Brand and
  water. Add pudding mix; beat well. Chill until
  thickened, about 20 minutes.

2 Fold in whipped cream.

3 Spoon 1 cup (250 mL) pudding mixture into
  2 1/2 quart (2.5 L) glass serving bowl*. Top with
  one third each of wafers, bananas and pudding.
  Repeat layering twice, ending with pudding.
  Cover; Chill 4 hours or overnight.

.

*Can also be layered in individual serving dishes.

PREP TIME: 15 minutes
plus chilling time
SERVINGS: 10-12

Mousses, Pudding & Trifles

Fudge & Candy

It's fun to make candy – especially if you succeed! Because Eagle Brand is milk and sugar boiled down to a creamy-rich consistency, the tedious part has been done for you. Fudge and candies turn out creamier and smoother... perfect.

Chocolate fudge is Eagle Brand at its absolute easiest and dreamiest. From after-school treats to holiday gifts, your friends and family will hardly believe you made it yourself. Or, create elegant white or dark chocolate truffles rolled in cocoa powder, icing sugar or finely crushed nuts.

Eagle Brand, icing sugar and flavouring make the fondant-like filling in chocolate-dipped Easter Eggs and filled candies. Peanut butter, marshmallows, fruit flavours, and the caramel that Eagle Brand does best are all ingredients found at the centre of an Eagle Brand confection.

Savour these timeless treasures and sweet surprises... made with the magic of Eagle Brand.

Super Chocolate Fudge

Since 'Magic French Fudge' in the 1920s, Eagle Brand has been making fudge foolproof and fun, with as many variations as you have imagination! Here's the basic recipe…have fun!

PREP TIME: 10 minutes plus chilling time
SERVINGS: 64-1" squares

3 cups (750 mL) semi-sweet chocolate chips
1 can (300 mL) **Regular Eagle Brand®**
2 tsp (10 mL) vanilla extract
1/2 cup (125 mL) chopped nuts

1 Melt chocolate chips with Eagle Brand.

2 Remove from heat; stir in vanilla and nuts.

3 Spread evenly in parchment paper-lined 8 " (20 cm) square pan. Chill 4 hours or until firm. Remove from pan and cut into squares.

Bittersweet Chocolate Fudge :
Use bittersweet chocolate chips and hazelnuts.

Smooth & Silky Fudge:
Reduce chocolate to 2 cups (500 mL) in Step 1; stir in 1 1/4 cups (300 mL) icing sugar in Step 2; Reduce vanilla to 1 tsp (5 mL).

Ginger fudge :
Use dark chocolate; add 1/4 cup (50 mL) finely chopped crystallized ginger and a pinch of salt in Step 1; Reduce vanilla to 1 tsp (5 mL).

Rainbow Marshmallow Fudge:
Fold in 2 cups (500 mL) miniature coloured marshmallows in Step 2.

TIP:

For a richer fudge, melt chocolate with 2 tbsp (30 mL) butter. To bring out even more chocolatey flavour, add a pinch of salt to the melted chocolate.

Sucre à la Crème

Thank you to Québec for this sweet 'n creamy melt-in-your-mouth soft brown sugar fudge. With added maple sweetness, it's a true Canadian classic.

1 can (300 mL) **Regular Eagle Brand**®
1/2 cup (125 mL) maple syrup
1 cup (250 mL) brown sugar
1 tbsp (15 mL) butter
1/2 cup (125 mL) chopped nuts (optional)

1 Combine Eagle Brand with maple syrup, brown sugar and butter. Cook and stir over low heat until mixture becomes a rich brown colour, about 20 minutes or until a small amount of the mixture forms a soft ball when dropped in cold water.

2 Remove from heat and stir in nuts.

3 Spread mixture into parchment paper-lined 8 x 8" (2 L) square pan. Cool completely and cut into squares.

PREP TIME: 20-25 minutes
SERVINGS: 64-1" squares

Chocolate Snowswirl Fudge

2 cups (500 mL) miniature marshmallows
4 tbsp (60 mL) butter, divided
3 cups (750 mL) semi-sweet chocolate chips
1 can (300 mL) **Regular Eagle Brand**®
1 1/2 tsp (7.5 mL) vanilla extract
Pinch salt
1 cup (250 mL) chopped nuts (optional)

1 On low heat, melt marshmallows with 2 tbsp (30 mL) butter, stirring occasionally. Remove from heat and set aside.

2 Melt chocolate chips with Eagle Brand, the remaining 2 tbsp (30 mL) butter, vanilla and salt. Remove from heat; stir in nuts, if desired. Spread evenly into parchment paper-lined 8 or 9" (2-2.5 L) square pan.

3 Spread marshmallow mixture on top of fudge. With table knife or metal spatula, swirl through top of fudge.

4 Chill at least 2 hours or until firm. Lift from pan, peel off paper and cut into squares.

PREP TIME: 10 minutes
plus chilling time
SERVINGS: 64-1" squares

TIP:
There are 3 main ways to buy chocolate – in squares, in bulk blocks or as baking chips. To understand the conversion between them... 1 square of baking chocolate weighs 1 oz/28.4 g ... 1 cup/250 mL chocolate chips = 6 squares or 6 oz/170 g baking chocolate.

Fudge & Candy

Creamy White Fudge

PREP TIME: 10 minutes plus chilling time
SERVINGS: 64-1" squares

1 1/2 lb (680 g) white baking chocolate or confectioners' coating*
1 can (300 mL) **Regular Eagle Brand®**
Pinch salt
1 1/2 tsp (7.5 mL) vanilla extract
1 cup (250 mL) chopped nuts

1 Melt chocolate with Eagle Brand and salt.

2 Remove from heat; stir in vanilla and nuts.

3 Spread evenly onto parchment paper-lined 8 or 9" (2-2.5 L) square pan. Chill 2 hours or until firm. Peel off paper and cut into squares. Store tightly covered at room temperature.

White Praline Fudge:

Omit vanilla. Add 1 tsp (5 mL) maple flavouring and use chopped pecans.

Confetti Fudge:

Omit nuts. Add 1 cup (250 mL) chopped mixed candied fruit.

Rum Raisin Fudge:

Omit vanilla. Add 1 1/2 tsp (7.5 mL) white vinegar, 1 tsp (5 mL) rum extract and 3/4 cup (175 mL) raisins.

White Chocolate Cherry Nut Fudge (shown):

Reduce nuts to 1/2 cup (125 mL) add 1/2 cup (125 mL) maraschino cherries.

TIP:

White confectioners' coating can be purchased in bakeshops and bulk food stores. It is also called white coating wafers.

Holiday Jewel Fudge

2 cups (500 mL) white chocolate chips
1 can (300 mL) **Regular Eagle Brand®**
1 tsp (5 mL) vanilla extract
1/2 cup (125 mL) icing sugar, sifted
1/2 cup (125 mL) pistachios, toasted and chopped
1/3 cup (75 mL) chopped dried cranberries

1 Melt chocolate chips with Eagle Brand; cook for 15 minutes, stirring frequently.

2 Remove from heat, stir in vanilla. Stir in icing sugar and beat 1 minute.

3 Stir in pistachios and cranberries.

4 Spread evenly into parchment-lined 8" (2 L) baking pan. Cover and chill for 3 hours; cut into squares.

PREP TIME: 20 minutes
plus chilling time
SERVINGS: 64-1" squares

TIP:

Always melt chocolate over low heat using a heavy bottom pot, or double boiler, or in the microwave on 50% power stirring often. The more finely chopped the chocolate or smaller the chip, the more evenly it will melt.

Keylime Fudge

3 cups (750 mL) white chocolate chips
1 can (300 mL) **Regular Eagle Brand®**
2 tsp (10 mL) finely shredded lime peel
2-3 tbsp (30-45 mL) key lime or regular lime juice
1 cup (250 mL) chopped macadamia nuts, toasted

1 Melt chocolate with Eagle Brand over low heat until smooth.

2 Remove from heat. Stir in lime peel and lime juice. Stir in nuts.

3 Spread mixture evenly into parchment paper-lined 8 x 8" (2 L) pan. Cover and chill two hours or until firm. Cut into squares.

PREP TIME: 15 minutes
plus chilling time
SERVINGS: 64-1" squares

TIP:

To toast chopped nuts, spread them in a single layer in a shallow baking pan. Bake in a preheated 350°F (180°C) oven 5 -10 minutes or until light golden brown, stirring them up frequently to ensure even browning on all sides.

Fudge & Candy

Cookies n' Dream Fudge

PREP TIME: 10 minutes plus chilling time
SERVINGS: 64-1" squares

3 pkgs (170 g each) white baking chocolate, chopped
1 can (300 mL) **Regular Eagle Brand®**
Pinch salt
2 cups (500 mL) coarsely crushed chocolate crème-filled sandwich cookies

1 Melt chocolate with Eagle Brand and salt.

2 Remove from heat. Stir in crushed cookies.

3 Spread into parchment paper-lined 8 x 8 " (2 L) square pan. Chill 2 hours or until firm. Cut into squares.

Magical Fudge Clusters (shown above)

PREP TIME: 10 minutes
plus chilling time
SERVINGS: 1-1/2 lb (750 g)

2 cups (500 mL) brown sugar
2 cups (500 mL) granola cereal
1/2 cup (125 mL) butter, softened
1 tsp (5 mL) vanilla extract
1 can (300 mL) **Regular Eagle Brand®**, caramelized*

1 Combine all ingredients and bring to a boil, stirring constantly. Simmer, stirring constantly, until mixture is well combined and sugar has dissolved.

2 Spread in parchment paper-lined 8 x 8 " (2 L) square pan. Cool thoroughly. Cut into squares.

*See p. 128 for 3 ways to caramelize Eagle Brand.

Holiday Fondant Fudge Log

PREP TIME: 15 minutes plus setting and chilling time
SERVINGS: 4 logs (about 56 pieces)

1 can (300 mL) **Regular Eagle Brand**®
1 3/4 cups (425 mL) icing sugar
2 tbsp (30 mL) finely grated orange rind
2 pkgs (170 g each) bittersweet or semi-sweet
   chocolate squares, coarsely chopped
1 tbsp (15 mL) corn syrup
1/2 tsp (2.5 mL) vanilla extract
Optional coatings : chocolate or multi-coloured
   sprinkles, finely chopped nuts, flaked coconut

1 Beat 1/3 cup (75 mL) Eagle Brand with sugar and
orange rind until smooth and thick. Turn fondant
mixture out onto surface sprinkled with icing sugar.
Knead lightly into a ball; divide into 4 equal parts. Roll
each into a 6 " (15 cm) log.

2 Melt together remaining Eagle Brand, chocolate, corn
syrup and vanilla. Remove from heat; stir until smooth.

3 Spread 1/4 of chocolate mixture onto a large piece of
waxed paper, to a 7x4-inch (18x10 cm) rectangle.
Place fondant log in centre. Repeat with remaining
chocolate mixture and fondant. Let stand 15 minutes
at room temperature.

4 Using waxed paper, tightly roll up each side of fudge
layer to completely enclose fondant log. Roll logs in
coating of choice, if using. Wrap tightly in waxed paper
and chill until firm, about 1 hour. Cut into 1/4" (.5 cm)
rounds to serve. Store refrigerated, well-wrapped for
up to 3 weeks.

Ginger filled:
Omit orange rind in fondant.
Add 1/4 cup (50 mL) finely
   chopped crystallized ginger for
   a full recipe; 1 tbsp (15 mL)
   for a quarter.

Nut filled:
Omit orange rind in fondant.
Add 1/4 cup (50 mL) finely
   chopped toasted almonds and
   1/4 tsp (1 mL) almond extract
   for a full recipe; 1 tbsp (15 mL)
   almonds and a dash almond
   extract for a quarter.

Peppermint:
Omit orange rind in fondant.
   Add 1 tsp (5 mL) peppermint
   extract for a full recipe; 1/4 tsp
   (1 mL) for a quarter.

Orange filled:
2 tbsp (30 mL) finely grated
   orange rind for a full recipe;
   1 1/2 tsp (7.5 mL) for a quarter
   recipe.

Classic Chocolate Truffles

Creamy confections to win the heart ... that's what you and Eagle Brand do best together !

PREP TIME: 15 minutes
plus chilling time
SERVINGS: about 5 dozen

3 pkgs (175 g each) semi-sweet chocolate chips
1 can (300 mL) **Regular Eagle Brand**®
1 tbsp (15 mL) vanilla extract
Optional Coatings: finely chopped nuts, flaked
  coconut, chocolate sprinkles, coloured sprinkles,
  unsweetened cocoa powder, icing sugar

1 Melt chocolate chips with Eagle Brand.

2 Remove from heat and stir in vanilla.
Chill 3 hours or until firm.

3 Shape into 1" (2.5 cm) balls; roll in any of the
coatings. Chill again until firm.

Heavenly Hazelnut Truffles

PREP TIME: 20 minutes
plus chilling time
SERVINGS: about 6 dozen

1 cup (250 mL) semi-sweet chocolate chips
1 can (300 mL) **Regular Eagle Brand**®
1 1/4 cups (300 mL) hazelnut spread*
1 tsp (5 mL) hazelnut liqueur or vanilla extract
  (optional)
Whole hazelnuts (optional)
Coating: Cocoa powder or ground hazelnuts

1 Melt chocolate with Eagle Brand and hazelnut
spread. Remove from heat and stir in liqueur.
Chill until firm.

2 Shape into 1" (2.5 cm) balls. Or, form about
1 tbsp (15 mL) of mixture around a hazelnut then
shape into a ball. Roll in cocoa powder or finely
chopped nuts.

*Contains peanut oil

TIP:
We recommend using Regular Eagle Brand for fudge, truffles and any confection which needs to
hold a shape.

Make 'em Melt White Chocolate Truffles

PREP TIME: 30 minutes plus chilling time
SERVINGS: about 5 dozen

1 1/2 lb (680 g) white chocolate, chopped
1 can (300 mL) **Regular Eagle Brand®**
1 tbsp (15 mL) orange liqueur or vanilla extract
Optional coatings: finely shredded coconut, finely chopped nuts, chocolate sprinkles, coloured sprinkles, gold flakes, unsweetened cocoa powder, icing sugar

1 Melt 1 lb (454 g) chocolate with Eagle Brand. Remove from heat; stir in liqueur. Chill 3 hours or until firm.

2 Shape into 1 " (2.5 cm) balls; place on wax paper-lined trays. Chill until firm.

3 Melt remaining white chocolate. Dip truffles in melted chocolate and roll in coatings of choice. Place back on paper-lined tray. Chill.

TIP:
To ensure an evenly shaped truffle, keep hands cool by immersing frequently in cold water. Dry thoroughly before touching the chocolate. Or, use a melon baller to shape perfect truffles.

Layered Mint Chocolate Candy

An ideal after-dinner confection, these simple but sophisticated treats are perfect boxed as a homemade St. Patrick's Day gift!

PREP TIME: 15 minutes
plus chilling time
SERVINGS: 1 3/4 lbs (875 g) candy

10 squares (1 oz/28 g each) semi-sweet chocolate
1 can (300 mL) **Regular Eagle Brand®**
2 tsp (10 mL) vanilla extract
1 pkg (170 g) white baking chocolate
1 tbsp (15 mL) peppermint extract
Few drops green food colour (optional)

1 Melt semi-sweet chocolate with 1 cup (250 mL) Eagle Brand. Remove from heat and stir in vanilla.

2 Spread half the mixture into a parchment paper-lined 8 " (20 cm) square pan. Chill 10 minutes until firm. Hold remaining chocolate at room temperature.

3 Melt white chocolate with remaining Eagle Brand. Stir in peppermint extract and food colour. Spread on chilled chocolate layer. Chill 10 minutes or until firm.

4 Spread reserved chocolate mixture on mint layer. Chill 2 hours. Lift from pan and peel off paper. Cut into squares.

Milk Chocolate Brandy Balls

PREP TIME: 25 minutes
plus chilling time
SERVINGS: about 6 dozen candies

3 cups (750 mL) vanilla wafer cookie crumbs
5 tbsp (75 mL) brandy
1 pkg (300 g) milk chocolate chips
1 can (300 mL) **Regular Eagle Brand®**
1 cup (250 mL) finely-chopped nuts or coconut
    or 1/2 cup (125 mL) cocoa

1 Combine crumbs and brandy. Set aside.

2 In heavy saucepan, over low heat, melt chocolate. Remove from heat; stir in Eagle Brand. Gradually add crumb mixture; mix well. Chill 30 minutes.

3 Shape into 3/4 " (1.8 cm) balls; roll in nuts or sprinkle with sifted cocoa.

Note: Flavour of these candies improves after 24 hours. They can be made ahead, wrapped well and stored in freezer.

Maple Candy Balls

PREP TIME: 25 minutes plus chilling time
SERVINGS: 120 candies

1 can (300 mL) **Regular Eagle Brand**®
1/4 cup (60 mL) butter, softened
2 tbsp (30 mL) maple extract
1 1/2 cups (375 mL) chopped nuts
1 pkg (1 kg) icing sugar
1 1/2 lbs (750 g) semi-sweet
  chocolate, chopped

1 Mix together Eagle Brand, butter, maple extract and nuts. Gradually beat in sugar. Chill in refrigerator for 3-4 hours (or for up to 2 days).

2 Roll into 1" (2.5 cm) balls. Keep refrigerated until ready to dip.

3 Melt chocolate in top of double boiler. Dip balls into chocolate. Place on parchment paper-lined baking sheets until set.

TIP:
Resting on tines of a fork or candy dipper, immerse any kind of candy centre, truffle or fondant egg into melted chocolate or confectioners' coating. Lift out and draw fork lightly against rim of bowl to remove excess chocolate.

Festive Snowballs Classic

The 1960s gave us the Barbie doll, a walk on the moon, and these delightful confections, perfect for gift-giving.

PREP TIME: 15 minutes
plus chilling time
SERVINGS: 36-48 snowballs

1 can (300 mL) **Regular Eagle Brand**®
1 tsp (5 mL) vanilla extract
1/3 cup (75 mL) maraschino cherries, quartered
30 marshmallows, cut in quarters
1/2 cup (125 mL) chopped nuts of choice
2 cups (500 mL) graham or vanilla wafer crumbs
2 1/2 cups (625 mL) flaked coconut

1 Combine Eagle Brand, vanilla, maraschino cherries, marshmallows, nuts and graham wafer crumbs; mix well.

2 Place coconut into a shallow bowl. With damp fingers, roll marshmallow mixture into 3/4″ balls and roll in coconut. Place onto cookie sheets lined with parchment or waxed paper. Chill 4 hours or until set.

Tropical Candy Clusters

PREP TIME: 15 minutes
SERVINGS: about 5 dozen

1 pkg (300 g) milk chocolate chips
1 pkg (170 g) semi-sweet chocolate chips
1 can (300 mL) **Regular Eagle Brand**®
1/4 tsp (1 mL) salt
1 1/2 cups (375 mL) coarsely chopped toasted almonds or macadamia nuts
1 cup (250 mL) chopped candied pineapple
2/3 cup (150 mL) flaked coconut

1 Melt both chocolate chips with Eagle Brand and salt.

2 Remove from heat; stir in remaining ingredients.

3 Drop by heaping teaspoonfuls onto wax paper-lined baking sheets; chill 2 hours or until firm.

TIP:

You can measure coconut by volume or weight. 1 cup (250 mL) flaked coconut = 100 g of any type of shredded coconut.

Coconut Rum Balls

3 cups (750 mL) vanilla wafer cookie crumbs
1 1/3 cups (325 mL) flaked coconut
1 cup (250 mL) finely chopped nuts
1 can (300 mL) **Regular Eagle Brand**®
1/4 cup (50 mL) rum
Additional flaked coconut

1 Combine crumbs, coconut and nuts.

2 Add Eagle Brand and rum; mix well. Chill 4 hours.

3 Shape into about 1 " (2.5 cm) balls. Roll in additional coconut.

Note: The flavour of these candies improves after 24 hours. They can be made ahead, covered and stored in the refrigerator for several weeks.

PREP TIME: 10 minutes plus chilling time
SERVINGS: 8 dozen

Chipper Peanut Candy

1 pkg (170 g) butterscotch or semi-sweet chocolate chips
1 can (300 mL) **Regular Eagle Brand**®
1 cup (250 mL) peanut butter
2 cups (500 mL) crushed potato chips
1 cup (250 mL) coarsely chopped peanuts

1 Melt chocolate chips with Eagle Brand and peanut butter; stir until well blended.

2 Remove from heat. Add potato chips and peanuts; mix well.

3 Press into a parchment paper-lined 8 or 9 " (2-2.5 L) square pan. Chill 2 hours or until firm. Cut into squares.

PREP TIME: 10 minutes plus chilling time
SERVINGS: 64-1" squares

Microwave Method: In 2-quart (2.2 L) glass measure, combine Eagle Brand, chocolate chips and peanut butter. Microwave on HIGH 4 minutes, stirring after 2 minutes. Proceed with step 2 above.

Fudge & Candy

Homemade Vanilla Caramels Classic

A classic Eagle Brand recipe from 1935... nothing makes caramel better !

PREP TIME: 20 minutes
SERVINGS: 64-1" or 32
oversized caramels

1 cup (250 mL) sugar
1 can (300 mL) **Regular Eagle Brand**®
1 tbsp (15 mL) butter
1/2 tsp (2.5 mL) vanilla extract

1 Place sugar in a heavy saucepan over low heat. Cook, brushing down sides of pan occasionally until melted and the colour of maple syrup. Do not stir, as it may cause crystallization.

2 Whisk in Eagle Brand and butter. Cook over low heat about 15 minutes, whisking constantly until mixture forms a soft ball (at about 240°F/115°C) when tested in cold water.

3 Remove from heat; add vanilla. Turn at once into a parchment paper-lined 8"x 8" (2 L) baking pan. Cool completely. Cut into squares.

Caramel Corn

PREP TIME: 20 minutes
SERVINGS: 5 cups (1.25 L)

2 cups (500 mL) brown sugar
1 cup (250 mL) light corn syrup
1/2 cup (125 mL) butter
1 can (300 mL) **Regular or Low Fat Eagle Brand**®
5 cups (1.25 mL) prepared popcorn
1 1/2 cups (375 mL) unsalted peanuts (optional)

1 Combine brown sugar, corn syrup and butter. Bring to a boil on medium high heat.

2 Add Eagle Brand, stirring continuously until it boils. Cook 5-10 minutes for caramel, scraping down sides intermittently, or cook to soft ball stage for more caramel taste and thicker caramel.

3 Pour caramel coating over popcorn in a large bowl, and toss quickly to coat. Add peanuts and toss again, if using. Cool. Chill if desired.

Ghostly Good Caramel Apples

16 small apples
16 wooden sticks
2 cups (500 mL) brown sugar
1 can (300 mL) **Regular Eagle Brand**®
1 cup (250 mL) golden corn syrup
1/2 cup (125 mL) butter
1 tsp (5 mL) vanilla extract
2-2 1/2 cups (500-625 mL) rice cereal
   or chopped peanuts

1 Wash and dry apples. Remove stems and insert
   a wooden stick into the stem end of each apple;
   set aside.

2 Combine brown sugar, Eagle Brand, corn syrup
   and butter. Gently simmer mixture, stirring constantly
   over medium heat, about 15 minutes. Remove from
   heat, stir in vanilla.

3 Working quickly, dip each apple into the hot caramel
   mixture (use a spoon if necessary to spread mixture
   evenly over apples). Allow excess mixture to drip off. Dip
   bottoms of apples into cereal or peanuts. Place on
   parchment paper-lined baking sheet; let stand until
   firm, about 25 minutes.

PREP TIME: 35 minutes
plus setting time
SERVINGS: 16 apples

Petits Cornets

1 can (300 mL) **Regular Eagle Brand**®
2 cups (500 mL) packed brown sugar
1/3 cup (75 mL) corn syrup
1/2 cup (125 mL) butter, cut into pieces
2 cups (500 mL) mini marshmallows
40 small cornets or miniature ice cream cones

1 In large glass bowl, combine Eagle Brand, brown
   sugar, corn syrup and butter. Cook in microwave
   on High (100%) for 6 minutes, stirring every
   2 minutes.

2 Stir in marshmallows. Cook in microwave on High
   (100%) for 2 minutes, stirring every 30 seconds.

3 Pour mixture into cornets. Stand upright in glasses
   or popsicle holders. Chill 1 hour.

PREP TIME: 15 minutes
plus chilling time
SERVINGS: 40 mini cornets

Fudge & Candy

Merry Christmas Mice

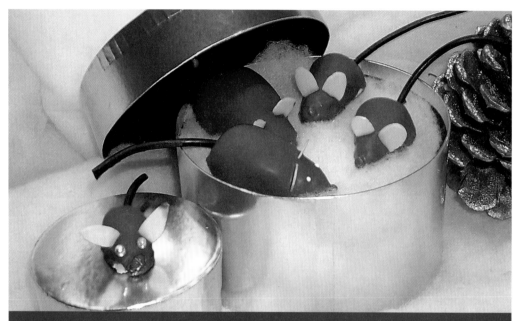

PREP TIME: 30 minutes plus chilling and decorating time
SERVINGS: 30 egg-sized mice

1/2cup (125 mL) butter, softened
1 tsp (5 mL) salt
1 can (300 mL) **Regular Eagle Brand**®
1 tsp (5 mL) vanilla, mint or almond extract
2.2 lb (1 kg) icing sugar
1.5 lb (680 g) semi-sweet or milk chocolate, melted
Slivered almonds

Decorations:
Licorice whip, cut into 3-4" (7-10 cm) lengths
Miniature candy covered chocolate pieces or sugar eyes
Candy sprinkles (optional)

1 Cream butter and salt until fluffy. Beat in Eagle Brand and extract. Slowly beat in icing sugar until well blended.

2 Knead with hands until mixture is smooth and pliable.

3 Form mixture into egg sized teardrop-shaped "mice". Place onto wax paper lined tray. Cover and chill 4 hours or until firm.

4 Using a piece of licorice whip, make a hole for the tail in the fat end of the mouse. Remove licorice. Dip mice in chocolate. Place back on tray.

5 Decorate with licorice whip as a tail, almonds as ears and miniature candy covered chocolate pieces or sugar eyes for a nose and eyes. Use sprinkles as fur if desired.

TIP:

Instead of candy covered chocolate pieces for the eyes, use sugar eyes found at most cake supply stores.

Sunny Chocolate Easter Eggs

Nothing but Eagle Brand could make these fondant-filled Easter Eggs so melt-in-your-mouth delicious. For delectable homemade gifts, decorate your eggs with tubel icing, sprinkles and candies, and wrap them in cello.

PREP TIME: 40 minutes plus chilling time
SERVINGS: 30 eggs

1/2 cup (125 mL) butter, softened
1 tsp (5 mL) salt
1 can (300 mL) **Regular Eagle Brand®**
1 tsp (5 mL) vanilla or almond extract
Few drops yellow food colouring
2.2 lbs (1 kg) icing sugar
1.5 lb (680 g) semi-sweet chocolate, melted
Decorative icing (pink, blue, green yellow)
Candy sprinkles

Flavoured eggs:

Substitute 1 tsp (5 mL) orange, cherry or mint extract for vanilla.

1 Cream butter and salt until fluffy. Gradually beat in Eagle Brand, vanilla and food colouring. Slowly beat in icing sugar until well blended.

2 Knead with hands until mixture is smooth and pliable. Form mixture into eggs. Place onto wax paper-lined tray. Cover and chill 4 hours, or until firm.

3 Resting each egg on a 2-pronged fork, dip into melted chocolate, letting excess coating drip off. Place back on wax paper-lined tray; let stand until firm.

4 Decorate with sprinkles or let chocolate stand until firm and decorate with icing.

TIP:

Top your Easter Eggs with your own homemade Royal Icing…Whisk together 3 cups (750 mL) icing sugar with 1/4 cup (50 mL) water for piped icing. Divide icing into smaller bowls and tint with several drops of food colouring, as desired. (Makes 3 cups)

Ice Cream & Frozen

Ever think you could make your own luscious, creamy homemade ice cream – without all the stirring, cooling and cooking – and without an ice cream maker?

With only 3 ingredients and 10 minutes prep time, you can make Eagle Brand's basic Vanilla Ice Cream. Then add your favourite ingredients for maximum indulgence. How about chocolate, strawberry or other fruit ice cream? Or swirls of fruit or butterscotch, chunks of chocolate, chopped cherries, crushed cookies or crunchy nuts? Because Eagle Brand has a very low freezing point, you will get a silky smooth texture and no ice crystals.

Eagle Brand also makes creamy cool frozen desserts, parfaits and cheesecakes for a light and sophisticated alternative for the holiday table and summer barbecues. And you and your kids can have fun making your own frosty frozen pops – with fruit juice, chocolate or even pudding.

From entertaining to summer fun, Eagle Brand has dozens of ways to a big ice creamy smile!

Eagle Brand Ice Cream

Eagle Brand makes the easiest ice cream ever! Start with the basic recipe for Vanilla and then go to town inventing your next indulgence. And no ice cream maker required!

PREP TIME: 5 minutes plus freezing time
SERVINGS: 6-8

1 can (300 mL) **Regular or Low Fat Eagle Brand®**
2 tbsp (30 mL) vanilla extract
2 cups (500 mL) whipping cream, whipped (DO NOT use non-dairy whipped topping)

1 Combine Eagle Brand and vanilla.

2 Fold in whipped cream.

3 Pour into 9 x 5-inch (2 L) loaf pan or other container; cover. Freeze 6 hours or until firm.

Butter Pecan:

Add 1-1 1/2 cups (250-375 mL) chopped pecans and
3 tbsp (45 mL) butter, melted to step 1. Substitute 1 tsp (5 mL) maple flavouring for vanilla extract.

Chocolate:

Add 2/3 cup (160 mL) chocolate syrup in step 1.

Cookies 'n Crème:

Add 1 cup (250 mL) coarsely crushed chocolate sandwich cookies (about 10 cookies) in step 2.

Mexican Chocolate:

Add 2/3 cup (160 mL) chocolate syrup, 1/2 tsp (2.5 mL) cinnamon and 1/8 tsp (.5 mL) cayenne in step 1. Add 1 tsp (5 mL) ground cinnamon in step 1

Fudge Swirl Supreme Ice Cream

2 cups (500 mL) whipping cream
1 can (300 mL) **Regular or Low Fat Eagle Brand**®
1/2 tsp (2.5 mL) vanilla extract
1 cup (250 mL) semi-sweet chocolate chips

1 Combine cream, 1/2 cup (125 mL) of the Eagle Brand and vanilla. Cover and chill 30 minutes.

2 Beat chilled mixture until soft peaks form. Spoon into 8-inch square (2 mL) baking pan. Cover and freeze
1 1/2 hours or until partially frozen.

3 Melt chips with remaining Eagle Brand. Cool 15 minutes. Swirl into partially frozen mixture. Cover and freeze 3 hours or until firm. Remove from freezer 10 minutes before serving.

PREP TIME: 25 minutes
plus freezing time
SERVINGS: 6-8

Maple Walnut Ice Cream

1 can (300 mL) **Regular or Low Fat Eagle Brand**®
1 cup (250 mL) chopped walnuts, toasted
1 tsp (5 mL) maple flavouring, or to taste
2 cups (500 mL) whipping cream, whipped

1 In large bowl, combine Eagle Brand, nuts and flavouring.

2 Fold in whipped cream.

3 Pour into 9 x 5″ (2 L) loaf pan or container; cover. Freeze 6 hours or until firm.

PREP TIME: 5 minutes
plus freezing time
SERVINGS: 6-8

Ice Cream

TIP:
Folding is a gentle mixing method, employing broad sweeping motions. You use the folding technique to gently combine light and airy mixtures, such as whipped cream or beaten egg whites, with a heavier mixture, to maintain as much of the air and volume as possible.

Mint Choco Chip Ice Cream

1 can (300 mL) **Regular or Low Fat Eagle Brand**®
2 tsp (10 mL) peppermint extract
3 drops green food colouring (optional)
2 tbsp (30 mL) water
2 cups (500 mL) whipping cream, whipped
1/2 cup (125 mL) mini semi-sweet chocolate chips

1 In a large bowl, combine Eagle Brand, peppermint extract, food colouring and water; mix well

2 Fold in whipped cream and chocolate chips.

3 Pour mixture into 9 X 5 " (2 L) loan pan or container. Cover and freeze 6 hours or until firm.

Café au Lait Ice Cream

1/2 cup (125 mL) hot water
4 tsp (20 mL) instant coffee crystals
2 cups (500 mL) whipping cream
1 can (300 mL) **Regular or Low Fat Eagle Brand**®
1/4 tsp (1 mL) almond extract
1/2 cup (125 mL) toasted chopped pecans or almonds (optional)

1 Stir together water and coffee crystals until dissolved; cool.

2 Add whipping cream, Eagle Brand and almond extract. Beat 7 minutes or until light and fluffy (mixture will mound but not hold peaks). Fold in nuts if desired.

3 Spoon into 8-inch (2 L) square baking pan or 9x5 " (2 L) loaf pan. Cover and freeze 4 hours or until firm.

Dulce de Leche Ice Cream

PREP TIME: 15 minutes plus freezing time
SERVINGS: 6-8

1 can (300 mL) **Regular or
Low Fat Eagle Brand**®
2 cups (500 mL) whipping cream,
whipped
2 tsp (30 mL) vanilla extract
1/2 cup (125 mL) toasted pecans,
chopped (optional)
1/4 cup (50 mL) Dulce de Leche
caramel, made to desired
consistency (see recipe p. 128)

1 Combine Eagle Brand and vanilla.

2 Fold in whipped cream.

3 Pour into 9 x 5-inch (2 L) loaf pan or other
container; cover. Freeze 2 hours.

4 Remove from freezer. Incorporate pecans and swirl
in the Dulche de Leche caramel. Freeze 4 hours
longer.

TIP:

Eagle Brand makes luscious caramel of any consistency, just by adding heat. See p. 128 for three
ways to caramelize Eagle Brand.

Fresh Fruit Ice Cream

1 can (300 mL)**Regular or Low Fat Eagle Brand**®
1 cup (250 mL) puréed or mashed fresh fruit
(peaches, strawberries, bananas, raspberries etc)
1 tbsp (15 mL) vanilla extract
2 cups (500 mL) whipping cream, whipped

1 In large bowl combine Eagle Brand and vanilla;
stir in 1 cup (250 mL) puréed fruit.

2 Fold in whipped cream.

3 Pour into 9x5" (2 L) loaf pan or other 2 quart
container; cover. Freeze 6 hours or until firm.

Banana Cinnamon: (shown)

Add 1 tsp (5 mL) ground cinnamon to Banana Ice
Cream in step 1.

Peach Amaretto:

Add 1/2 tsp (2.5 mL) amaretto or almond extract
to Peach Ice Cream.

Strawberry Cream Sorbet

2 pkgs (500 g each) frozen strawberries
1 can (300 mL)**Regular or Low Fat Eagle Brand**®
2/3 cup (150 mL) water

1 Let strawberries stand at room temperature for
15 minutes or until surface is slightly softened but
fruit is still frozen.

2 In blender container, combine Eagle Brand and
water. Gradually add strawberries; blending until
smooth. Serve immediately.

Peaches 'n Cream Sorbet:

Substitute frozen sliced peaches for strawberries.

Blackberry-Lemon Ice Cream

2 cups (500 mL) fresh or thawed frozen
  unsweetened blackberries, mashed
1 can (300 mL) **Regular or Low Fat Eagle Brand**®
1/4 cup (50 mL) lemon juice
1 tsp (5 mL) grated lemon rind, (optional)
3 cups (750 mL) 10% cream

1 In a large bowl, mash berries. Add Eagle Brand,
  lemon juice and rind, if desired; mix well.

2 Stir in cream.

3 Pour into 9 x 5 " (2 L) loaf pan or other
  container; cover. Freeze 6 hours or until firm.

PREP TIME: 10 minutes
plus freezing time
SERVINGS: 6-8

TIP:
Two cups (500 mL) fresh or thawed frozen unsweetened blueberries or raspberries can be substituted
for blackberries.

Strawberry Ripple Ice Cream

1 can (300 mL) **Regular or Low Fat Eagle Brand**®
1 tsp (5 mL) vanilla extract
2 cups (500 mL) whipping cream, whipped
1 cup (250 mL) fresh hulled or thawed frozen
  strawberries

1 In large bowl, combine Eagle Brand and extract. Fold
  in whipped cream.

2 Pour into 9 x 5 " (2 L) loaf pan or container.

3 Crush strawberries to desired consistency and drop
  by spoonfuls over the Eagle Brand mixture. With
  table knife, gently swirl strawberry mixture through
  out ice cream. Cover & freeze 6 hours or until firm.

PREP TIME: 10 minutes
plus freezing time
SERVINGS: 6-8

Minted Strawberry Ripple Ice Cream:
Use peppermint extract instead of vanilla.
Add a couple of drops of green food colouring in step 1, if desired.

Orange Dream Pops

PREP TIME: 10 minutes
plus freezing time
SERVINGS: 10 pops

3 cups (750 mL) orange juice
1 can (300 mL) **Regular or Low Fat Eagle Brand**®
1/4 cup (50 mL) lemon juice
10 5-oz paper cups *see tip below
10 wooden sticks

1 In large bowl, stir together orange juice, Eagle Brand and lemon juice. Pour into paper cups.

2 Cover each cup with foil. Make small hole in foil with knife. Insert wooden stick or plastic spoon into each cup through hole.

3 Freeze overnight or until firm. To serve, remove foil and paper cup.

Frozen Pudding Pops

PREP TIME: 15 minutes
plus freezing time
SERVINGS: 8 pops

1 can (300 mL) **Regular or Low Fat Eagle Brand**®
1 1/2 cups (375 mL) cold water
1 pkg (4 serving size) instant pudding and pie filing mix, any flavour
8 5-oz (155 mL) paper drink cups
8 wooden sticks

1 Combine Eagle Brand and water; mix well. Add pudding mix; beat well. Chill 5 minutes.

2 Pour equal portions into paper cups. Insert a wooden stick in centre of each pop; freeze 6 hours or until firm.

3 To serve, remove from freezer; let stand 5 minutes. Peel off paper cups.

Chocolate Peanut Butter Pops:

Beat Eagle Brand and 1/4 cup (50 mL) peanut butter until smooth. Gradually beat in water, then chocolate pudding mix. Proceed as above.

TIP:

Make your Pops in awesome shapes. For flat-bottomed pops, use small paper cups. To make cone shapes, use paper cups with pointed bottoms (set each cup in a foam cup or juice glass to keep it upright while freezing). For special decorative shapes, purchase an assortment of whimsical pop molds.

Ice Cream

Frozen Chocolate Banana Loaf

PREP TIME: 15 minutes plus freezing time
SERVINGS: 8-10

1 1/2 cups (375 mL) chocolate wafer cookie crumbs (about 30 wafers)
1/4 cup (50 mL) sugar
3 tbsp (45 mL) butter, melted
1 can (300 mL) **Regular or Low Fat Eagle Brand®**
2/3 cup (150 mL) chocolate-flavoured syrup
2 small ripe bananas, mashed (about 3/4 cup)
2 cups (500 mL) whipping cream, whipped (do not use non-dairy whipped topping)

1 Combine crumbs, sugar and butter; press firmly on bottom and halfway up sides of 9 x 5 " (2 L) parchment paper-lined loaf pan.

2 Combine Eagle Brand, syrup and bananas; mix well. Fold in whipped cream.

3 Pour into prepared pan; cover. Freeze 6 hours or until firm. To serve, lift from pan; peel off paper; serve immediately. Garnish as desired.

TIP:
Keep bananas from browning by brushing them with lemon or orange juice.

Fabulous Frozen Dessert Squares

Cool, tangy and fluffy… a sumptuous frozen Eagle Brand creation from ever-so-social 70s !

1 cup (250 mL) graham cracker crumbs
1/4 cup (50 mL) butter, melted
1/4 cup (50 mL) sugar
1 pkg (250 g) cream cheese, softened
1 can (300 mL) **Regular or Low Fat Eagle Brand**®
1/3 cup (75 mL) lemon juice
1 tsp (5 mL) vanilla extract
1 can (398 mL) whole berry cranberry sauce

PREP TIME: 10 minutes plus freezing time
SERVINGS: 8-10

1 Combine crumbs, butter and sugar. Press firmly onto bottom of 9″ (2.5L) square baking pan; chill.

2 Beat cream cheese until fluffy. Gradually beat in Eagle Brand until smooth. Stir in lemon juice and vanilla. Fold in cranberry sauce.

3 Pour mixture over prepared crust. Cover and freeze 6 hours or until firm. Cut into squares and garnish as desired.

Pineapple-Orange Variation:

Omit cranberry sauce. Fold in 1 can (398 mL) well-drained crushed pineapple and 1 tsp (5 mL) grated orange rind.

Frozen Mint Chocolate Mousse

A delicate, perfect ending to a perfect meal.

1 can (300 mL) **Regular or Low Fat Eagle Brand**®
2/3 cup (150 mL) chocolate syrup
1 tsp (5 mL) peppermint extract
1 cup (250 mL) whipping cream, whipped

1 In large bowl, combine Eagle Brand, syrup and peppermint extract. Fold in whipped cream.

2 Spoon equal portions into 6 or 8 individual serving dishes.

3 Freeze 3 to 4 hours or until firm. Garnish as desired. Serve immediately.

PREP TIME: 5 minutes plus chilling time
SERVINGS: 6-8

Ice Cream

Light Frozen Coffee Dessert Slices

PREP TIME: 15 minutes
SERVINGS: 8 to 10

1 tbsp (15 mL) instant coffee
3 tbsp (45 mL) water
1 can (300 mL) **Regular or Low Fat Eagle Brand**®
1/2 container (114 g) frozen light whipped dessert topping, thawed
30 to 36 reduced-fat vanilla wafers*
1/4 cup (50 mL) crushed reduced-fat vanilla wafers (about 10 wafers)*

*or use chocolate wafers to create a mocha flavour

1 Line bottom and edges of 8x4x2" (1.5 L) loaf pan with plastic wrap; set aside.

2 Dissolve coffee in water. In a medium bowl, combine 1 tbsp (15 mL) coffee mixture and Eagle Brand. Fold in dessert topping.

3 To assemble, layer 10 to 12 cookies on bottom of prepared pan, breaking up cookies as necessary to make an even layer. Drizzle with about 2 tbsp (30 mL) remaining coffee; let stand 2 minutes. Spoon 1 cup (250 mL) of the Eagle Brand mixture atop cookies in the pan. Repeat layering, allowing 2 minutes after each application of coffee. End with Eagle Brand mixture to coat all. Sprinkle with crushed cookie crumbs.

4 Cover and freeze 8 hours or until firm. Remove dessert from pan; remove plastic wrap and cut into slices.

TIP:

Drizzle chocolate on the plate and put ice cream slice on top. Garnish with chocolate-covered coffee beans, raspberries or pineapple slices. And there's always whipped cream, of course!

Candy Cane Frozen Mousse

1 pkg (225 g) cream cheese, softened
1 can (300 mL) **Regular or Low Fat Eagle Brand**®
1 cup (250 mL) crushed candy canes (peppermint, cinnamon or wintergreen)
2 cups (500 mL) whipping cream, whipped

1 In a large mixing bowl, beat cheese until fluffy. Gradually beat in Eagle Brand.

2 Stir in crushed candy. Fold in whipped cream.

3 Pour into serving dish, and cover. Freeze 6 hours or until firm. Can be made a few days ahead. Garnish as desired.

PREP TIME: 10 minutes plus freezing time
SERVINGS: 6-8

Toffee Frozen Mousse

Omit candy canes and use 1 cup (250 mL) toffee bits*.

*May contain almonds

Ice Cream

Pistachio Pineapple Parfaits

1 pkg (250 g) cream cheese, softened
1 can (300 mL) **Regular or Low Fat Eagle Brand**®
1/4 cup (50 mL) lime juice
1 pkg (4-serving size) instant pistachio pudding mix
1/2 cup (125 mL) toasted pistachio nuts or chopped pecans
1 cup (250 mL) crushed pineapple with juice
1 cup (250 mL) whipping cream, whipped

1 Beat cream cheese until fluffy. Add Eagle Brand; blend thoroughly. Stir in lime juice and pudding mix until smooth.

2 Stir in nuts and pineapple. Fold in whipped cream.

3 Pour into 6 parfait or dessert dishes.

4 Freeze 4 hours until firm. Garnish as desired.

PREP TIME: 15 minutes plus freezing time
SERVINGS: 6

Fruited Lime Freeze

PREP TIME: 10 minutes plus freezing time
SERVINGS: 9 servings

1 can (300 mL) **Regular or Low Fat Eagle Brand**®
1 cup (250 mL) sour cream
1/2 cup (125 mL) lime juice
1/2 cup (125 mL) fresh grapes, halved
OR
1 can (28 oz) fruit cocktail, well drained
1/2 cup (125 mL) chopped walnuts or almonds

1 Combine Eagle Brand, sour cream, and lime juice; mix well.

2 Stir in fruit and nuts.

3 Turn into ungreased 8x8 " (2 L) baking pan; freeze 5 hours or until firm. Remove from freezer 10 minutes before cutting.

TIP:
Eagle Brand has a very low freezing point and a low water content, so is ideal to make smooth and creamy frozen desserts that don't crystallize. Frozen desserts can be made ahead and frozen for up to a week.

Toppings, Sauces & Fondues

Here's the best magic trick of all … add a little heat, a little water, a little lemon or chocolate, and you can turn any dessert into a showpiece.

Add hot water to Eagle Brand – it's a creamy smooth sauce. Melt with cocoa and a bit of hot water – it's a wonderful frosting. Add lemon juice to Eagle Brand – get a light, tangy sauce. Mix it with icing sugar – elegant spreadable icing. Melt Eagle Brand with chocolate, maple syrup, coffee…for silky fondues to dip fruit or pound cake in.

And if that's not enough, Eagle Brand plus heat equals the richest, creamiest, most indulgent caramel you've ever tasted! Soft and flowing caramel for ice cream and cake toppings… thick and rich Dulce de Leche for dipping, and firmer still to make vanilla caramels or filled candies. We have 3 easy ways to caramelize Eagle Brand …oven, stovetop and microwave.

Top all your favourite desserts with added sweet surrender.

Hot Fudge Sauce *Classic*

One of the simplest and earliest discoveries of Eagle Brand magic, you can make this ahead and use it when the urge strikes... or bottle it for a sweet homemade gift.

PREP TIME: 5 minutes
SERVINGS: 2 cups (500 mL)

1 cup (250 mL) semi-sweet chocolate chips
1 can (300 mL) **Regular or Low Fat Eagle Brand®**
2 tbsp (30 mL) butter or margarine
2 tbsp (30 mL) water
1 tsp (5 mL) vanilla extract

1 Melt chocolate chips with Eagle Brand, butter and water. Beat smooth with wire whisk if necessary.

2 Remove from heat and stir in vanilla.

3 Serve warm over ice cream; or use as a fruit dipping sauce. Store leftovers covered in refrigerator, reheat to serve.

Spirited Hot Fudge Sauce:
Add 1/2 cup almond, coffee, mint or orange flavoured liqueur with the vanilla.

Creamy Pecan Rum Sauce

PREP TIME: 15 minutes
SERVINGS: 1 1/2 cups (375 mL)

1/4 cup (50 mL) butter
1 can (300 mL) **Regular or Low Fat Eagle Brand®**
1/2 tsp (2.5 mL) rum flavouring
Dash salt
1/4 cup (50 mL) chopped pecans

1 In heavy saucepan, over medium heat, melt butter; add remaining ingredients. Cook and stir until slightly thickened, 10 to 12 minutes (sauce thickens as it cools). Serve warm over baked apples, fruit or ice cream.

Microwave method : In 1-quart (1.14 L) glass measure, microwave butter on full power (high) 1 minute or until melted. Stir in remaining ingredients. Microwave on 2/3 power (medium high) 3 to 3/12 minutes. Proceed as above.

TIP:

To reheat sauces: In a small heavy saucepan combine desired amount of sauce with small amount of water. Over low heat, stir constantly until heated through.

Caramel Apple Topping

4 tbsp (60 mL) butter or margarine
4-5 medium eating apples, peeled and thinly sliced
   (4-5 cups)
1 can (300 mL) **Regular or Low Fat Eagle Brand®**,
   caramelized *

1 Melt butter in 10-inch(25 cm) skillet over medium
heat; stir in apples. Cook about 3 minutes, stirring
frequently, until tender.

2 Stir in caramel until warmed and well mixed.

PREP TIME: 10 minutes
plus caramelizing time*
SERVINGS: 3 cups (750 mL)

TIP:
*See page 128 for ways to make scrumptious caramel from Eagle Brand. Time depends on method used
and desired consistency of caramel.

Magic Fruit Cream Sauce Classic

*Tang up a cake or serve over a cottage cheese salad.
Creamy, fruity and smooth… since 1939 !*

PREP TIME: 5 minutes
SERVINGS: 2 cups (500 mL)

1/2 can (150 mL) Regular or Low Fat Eagle
   Brand®
1/2 cup (50 mL) lemon juice
1/2 tsp (2.5 mL) grated lemon rind
1 cup (250 mL) fruit or berries (strawberries,
   blueberries, raspberries, …drained crushed
   pineapple, chopped peaches or bing cherries…
   or chopped bananas)

1 Mix together Eagle Brand, lemon juice and lemon
rind. Stir until mixture thickens. Stir in fruit.

Warm Coffee Cascade

PREP TIME: 5 minutes
SERVINGS: 1 1/2 cups (375 mL)

3 tbsp (45 mL) brandy
2 tbsp (30 mL) instant coffee
   powder
1 can (300 mL) **Regular or Low
   Fat Eagle Brand®**

1 Warm brandy over medium heat.

2 Remove from heat; stir in coffee
and Eagle Brand.

3 Serve warm, if desired.

Toppings, Sauces & Fondues

Creamy Strawberry Lime Dressing

4 tbsp (60 mL) strawberry jam
1/2 can (150 mL) **Regular or Low Fat Eagle Brand**®
1 cup (250 mL) sour cream
1-2 tsp (5-10 mL) lime juice

1 In a medium bowl, whisk jam untill smooth.

2 Add remaining ingredients; whisk until smooth. Cover; chill to hold.

3 Allow to come to room temperature before serving. Serve with fresh fruit.

Lemon Crème

All the rage in the roaring 20s, this sweet and tangy sauce tops everything from fruit to cake, trifles to bread pudding… all in 3 minutes prep time!

PREP TIME: 3 minutes
SERVINGS: 1 1/2 cups (375 mL)

1 can (300 mL) **Regular or Low Fat Eagle Brand**®
1/2 cup (125 mL) lemon juice
1 tsp (5 mL) grated lemon rind (optional)
4 drops yellow food colouring (optional)

1 Stir together Eagle Brand and lemon juice. Stir in food colouring, if desired.

2 Use immediately or store covered in refrigerator.

TIP:

Individual Berries and Crème Trifles: Stir together 2 cups (500 mL) angel cake cubes and 1 cup (250 mL) fresh berries. Divide among 4 dessert dishes. Spoon Lemon Crème or Creamy Strawberry Lime Dressing atop each. Serves 4.

Toppings, Sauces & Fondues

Lemon Cream Cheese Icing

1 can (300 mL) **Regular or Low Fat Eagle Brand**®
2 egg yolks
3 tbsp (45 mL) lemon juice
1 tsp (5 mL) vanilla extract
Yellow food colouring, optional
1 pkg (225 g) cream cheese

1 Combine Eagle Brand, egg yolks and lemon juice. Over medium heat, cook and stir rapidly until thickened and bubbly, 4- 5 minutes. Remove from heat; stir in vanilla and food colouring, if desired. Chill 1 hour.

2 Beat cream cheese until fluffy. Gradually beat in lemon mixture until smooth.

NOTE: Use to frost one 8-or 9" two layer, one 13x9" two-layer, or 15x10-inch cake.

PREP TIME: 15 minutes
plus chilling time
SERVINGS: 2 1/2 cups (625 mL)

Eagle Brand® Chocolate Icing

PREP TIME: 8-12 minutes
SERVINGS: 1 1/2 cups (375 mL)

2 oz (57 g) semi-sweet or unsweetened chocolate
1 can (300 mL) **Regular Eagle Brand**®
Dash salt
3 tbsp (45 mL) water
1 tsp (5 mL) vanilla extract

1 Over medium heat, melt together chocolate, Eagle Brand and salt, stirring until chocolate melts and mixture thickens, about 6-8 minutes.

2 Remove from heat; stir in water and vanilla. Cook and stir rapidly until thickened again, about 2-4 minutes. Cool 10 minutes.

NOTE: Use to frost one 13x9-inch cake or 2 dozen cupcakes.

Eagle Brand® Spiced Frosting

PREP TIME: 5 minutes
SERVINGS: 1 3/4 cups (425 mL)

1 1/2 cups (375 mL) icing sugar
1 tbsp (15 mL) cocoa
1/2 tsp (2.5 mL) cinnamon
1/4 tsp (1 mL) cloves
1/4 tsp (1 mL) nutmeg
1/4 cup (50 mL) **Regular or Low Fat Eagle Brand**®
1/2 tsp (2.5 mL) vanilla extract

1 Stir together sugar and dry spices.

2 Add Eagle Brand and vanilla. Beat until smooth and creamy.

3 Spread on cold cake.

Fudgey Chocolate Fondue

Dip the treasures of summer in something sweet, simple and indulgent ! A classic from the fabulous 50s, this fondue can also be served warm or cold over ice cream.

PREP TIME: 10 minutes
SERVINGS: 3 1/4 cups (800 mL)

2 cups (500 mL) chocolate
  topping sauce
1 can (300 mL) **Regular or
  Low Fat Eagle Brand**®
Pinch salt
1 1/2 tsp (7 mL) vanilla extract
*Dippers

1 In heavy saucepan, combine chocolate sauce, Eagle Brand and salt. Over medium heat, cook and stir until mixture just comes to a boil.

2 Remove from heat; stir in vanilla.

3 Serve warm with dippers.

Maple Whiskey Fondue

Omit vanilla extract. Add 1/4 cup (50 mL) whiskey and 1 tsp (5 mL) maple extract in step 2.

Golden Chocolate Fondue:

Substitute chocolate sauce with 3 squares (1oz/28 g each) unsweetened chocolate, chopped. Melt with Eagle Brand and 1 cup (250 mL) caramel ice cream topping. Omit salt and vanilla extract.

TIP:

*Here are some ideas for dippers for your fondue: pound cake, lady fingers, apple slices, strawberries, pineapple or banana chunks, grapes, kiwi fruit.

Dulce de Leche Classic

Quite simply, 'the oldest trick in our book', heating Eagle Brand makes a thick, rich, luscious caramel. Perfect for dipping fruit, cake or cookies, or as a decadent topping for ice cream or cake.

1 can (300 mL) **Regular or Low Fat Eagle Brand**®

1 Pour Eagle Brand into a 9″ (23 cm) ovenproof plate. Cover with foil; place in large shallow baking pan, pour hot water into larger pan to depth of 1″ (2.5 cm). Bake in preheated 425°F (220 °C) oven 1 hour or until thick and caramel-coloured.

2 Beat warm Eagle Brand until smooth. Cool 1 hour.

PREP TIME: 5 minutes
plus baking and cooling time
SERVINGS: 1 1/4 cups (300 mL)

NOTE: See p. 128 for other convenient ways to caramelize Eagle Brand.
CAUTION: Never heat Eagle Brand in the can.

Dipsy Doodles Butterscotch Dip

1 (6-serving size) cooked butterscotch pudding mix (not instant)
1 can (300 mL) **Regular or Low Fat Eagle Brand**®
2 cups (500 mL) milk
Apples or pears, cored or sliced, or banana chunks

1 Combine pudding mix, Eagle Brand and milk. Cook and stir until just thickened and bubbly; cook 2 minutes more. Cool slightly.

2 Pour into serving bowl or individual cups. Serve warm with fruit.

PREP TIME: 10 minutes
SERVINGS: about 2 1/2 cups (625 mL)

TIP:
To prevent fresh apples or pears from browning, brush lightly with fresh lemon juice.

Toppings, Sauces & Fondues

Beverages

Before Eagle Brand became known as the "magic ingredient" in baking, it was known as a life-saving food and drink additive. The world first discovered how smoothly it blended with hot coffee, and combined with chocolate and hot water to make positively perfect hot chocolate.

From the 1940's on, the repertoire expanded and now the holidays have become synonymous with Eagle Brand's flavoured liqueurs, velvety nogs, spirited punches, and frozen bartender parfaits. Today, international inspirations include chocolatey Brazilian Coffee, Iced Coffee Frappés, Oriental Teas & Coffees, creamy Indian Chai Tea, Vietnamese Shakes and Caribbean Fruit Smoothies.

Eagle Brand is once again finding popularity in its beginnings as new trends turn beverages into sweet indulgences!

Creamy Hot Chocolate *Classic*

Our favourite comfort drink. And the oldest of our Eagle Brand classics, dating back to the 1860s.

PREP TIME: 10 minutes
SERVINGS: 8

1 can (300 mL) **Regular or Low Fat Eagle Brand**®
1/2 cup (125 mL) unsweetened cocoa powder
1 1/2 tsp (7.5 mL) vanilla or peppermint extract
1/8 tsp (.5 mL) salt
6 1/2 cups (1.6 L) boiled hot water
Marshmallows (optional)

1 In large saucepan, combine Eagle Brand cocoa, vanilla and salt; mix well.

2 Over medium heat, slowly stir in water; heat through, stirring occasionally. Top with marshmallows if desired.

Brazilian Coffee

PREP TIME: 10 minutes
SERVINGS: 8 cups

1/3 cup (75 mL) cocoa
1 tsp (5 mL) salt
1 tsp (5 mL) ground cinnamon
1 can (300 mL) **Regular or Low Fat Eagle Brand**®
5 cups (1.25 L) water
1 1/3 cups (325 mL) strong coffee

1 In a 3.5 L saucepan, combine cocoa, salt and cinnamon. Add Eagle Brand; mix well.

2 Over medium heat, slowly stir in water and coffee; heat thoroughly but do not boil. Serve immediately.

Beverages

My Chai Tea

PREP TIME: 10 minutes
SERVINGS: 4 cups (1 L)

4 cups (1 L) water
1 cinnamon stick
8 whole cloves
2 tea bags (orange pekoe variety)
1/4 cup (50 mL) **Regular or Low Fat Eagle Brand**®

1 In medium-sized saucepan, combine water and spices and bring to a boil; cover and simmer 5 minutes. Remove from heat.

2 Add tea bags; cover and let steep 4-5 minutes. Remove tea bags and spices. Stir in Eagle Brand.® Serve hot.

Oriental Milk Tea

Steeped black tea, poured from a pot
1-2 tsp (5-10 mL) per cup, **Regular or Low Fat Eagle Brand**®

1 Steep tea for the desired time, in a teapot.

2 Add Eagle Brand to each cup. Pour in hot tea and stir.

PREP TIME: 5 minutes plus steeping time

Thai Iced Coffee

PREP TIME: 5 minutes
SERVINGS: 1 cup (250 mL)

1/2 cup (125 mL) brewed coffee
1/2 cup (125 mL) boiling water
4 tsp (20 mL) **Regular or Low Fat Eagle Brand**®
Crushed ice

1 Blend ingredients together and pour over ice.

TIP:
Store unused Eagle Brand refrigerated in a sealed glass container for up to 10 days.

Café Frappé

PREP TIME: 5 minutes
SERVINGS: 4

1 can (300 mL) **Regular or Low Fat Eagle Brand**®
2 cups (500 mL) cold coffee
3/4 cup (175 mL) milk or cream
3 tbsp (45 mL) hazelnut or almond liqueur (optional)
2 tbsp (30 mL) chocolate syrup (optional)
Crushed ice, as needed

1 Place Eagle Brand coffee, milk, liqueur and syrup in blender container; blend until smooth.

2 Serve over crushed ice. Garnish as desired.

Raspberry Café Frappé:
Substitute 3 tbsp (45 mL) raspberry syrup or liqueur for nut liqueur.

Beverages

Eagle Brand® Fruit Shakes

The creamy magic of Eagle Brand plus the goodness of fresh fruit… in true 1950s diner style.

1 can (300 mL) Regular or Low Fat Eagle Brand®
1 cup (250 mL) cold water
1/3 cup (75 mL) lemon juice
*FRUIT as below
2 cups (500 mL) ice cubes

1 In blender container, combine all ingredients
except ice; blend well.

2 Gradually add ice, blending until smooth.
(Mixture stays thick and creamy stored in refrigerator.)

PREP TIME: 5 minutes
SERVINGS: 4

Banana Shake

2 ripe bananas, sliced.

Strawberry Shake

2 cups (500 mL) fresh strawberries, cleaned
and hulled or 2 cups (500 mL) frozen
unsweetened strawberries, partially thawed.

Pineapple Shake

1 can (225 g) crushed juice-packed
pineapple.

Strawberry Banana Shake

1 1/2 cup (375 mL) strawberries and
1/2 cup (125 mL) mashed bananas.

Orange Banana Shake

1 banana; use 1 cup (250 mL)
orange juice instead of water.

Banana Peanutty Shake

3 ripe bananas, sliced
3 tbsp (45 mL) smooth peanut butter or nut-free
pea butter*
1 cup (250 mL) cold water
1 can (300 mL) Regular or Low Fat Eagle Brand®
1/3 cup (75 mL) lemon juice
2 cups (500 mL) ice cubes

1 In blender container, combine all ingredients
except ice; blend well.

2 Gradually add ice, blending until smooth.

* Pea butter is a vegetable (pea) product made to
taste and look like peanut butter.

PREP TIME: 5 minutes
SERVINGS: 4

Berry Patch Smoothie

PREP TIME: 5 minutes
SERVINGS: 4

1 can (300 mL) **Regular or Low Fat Eagle Brand**®
1 1/2 cups (375 mL) cranberry juice
2 cups (500 mL) frozen raspberries
2 cups (500 mL) frozen strawberries

1 Place Eagle Brand and cranberry juice in blender container; blend until smooth.

2 Add frozen berries; continue to blend until well combined. Serve immediately. Garnish as desired.

Apple Pie Shake

PREP TIME: 5 minutes
SERVINGS: 4-5

1 can (300 mL) **Regular or Low Fat Eagle Brand**®, chilled
1 cup (250 mL) apple sauce, chilled
1/2 cup (125 mL) apple juice or apple cider, chilled
1/2 tsp (2.5 mL) apple pie spice*
2 cups (500 mL) crushed ice
Apple wedges and apple peel strips for garnish

1 In blender container, combine Eagle Brand, applesauce, apple juice and apple pie spice; cover and blend until smooth.

2 With blender running, gradually add ice, blending until smooth.

3 Serve immediately. Garnish with apple wedges and apple peel strips, if desired.

*Or substitute a mixture of 1/4 tsp (1 mL) ground nutmeg and a dash of ground allspice.

Sunshine Smoothie

PREP TIME: 5 minutes
SERVINGS: 4

1 can (300 mL) **Regular or Low Fat Eagle Brand**®
1 1/2 cups (375 mL) orange juice
1 1/2 cups (375 mL) chopped fresh peaches
1 1/2 cups (375 mL) chopped fresh mango
1-2 cups (250-500 mL) crushed ice or ice cubes

1 Place Eagle Brand, orange juice, peaches and mango in blender container; blend until smooth.

2 Add ice; continue to blend until well combined. Serve immediately. Garnish as desired.

Mango Cream

2 mangoes, peeled and chopped
1 can (300 mL) **Regular or Low Fat Eagle Brand**®
Ground nutmeg

1 Place mangoes and Eagle Brand in blender container; blend until smooth.

2 Serve sprinkled with nutmeg.

PREP TIME: 10 minutes
SERVINGS: 4

NOTE: Can be made ahead and refrigerated for up to 2 weeks.

Smooth 'n Sinful Irish Cream Liqueur

What better way to celebrate the magic of the season than to toast to friends with your own magical homemade liqueur. Perfect for gift-giving too !

PREP TIME: 5 minutes
SERVINGS: 4 cups (1 L)

1 can (300 mL) **Regular or Low Fat Eagle Brand**®
1 – 1 1/2 cups (250 to 375 mL) Irish whiskey*
1 cup (250 mL) table cream
1 tbsp (15 mL) chocolate syrup
1/2 tsp (2.5 mL) coconut extract (optional)

1 IIn blender container, combine Eagle Brand, whiskey, cream, syrup and coconut extract. Cover and blend until smooth.

2 Serve over crushed ice, if desired.

*1 cup (250 mL) cold coffee can be substituted in place of the Irish Whiskey.

Rum Cream Liqueur:
Omit Irish Whiskey. Use 1 to 1 1/2 cups (250-375 mL) rum.

Festive Eggnog

Classic

This satiny smooth holiday tradition spiced just right with vanilla and nutmeg murmurs perfection… with or without a touch of rum or brandy.

4 eggs, separated*
1 can (300 mL) **Regular or Low Fat Eagle Brand**®
1 cup (250 mL) brandy or rum (optional)
1 tsp (5 mL) vanilla extract
4 cups (1 L) homogenized milk
1/4 tsp (1 mL) salt
Nutmeg

1 In a large bowl beat egg yolks until thick and light. Gradually beat in Eagle Brand, brandy or rum, vanilla, milk and salt.

2 In a small bowl beat egg whites to soft peaks; gently fold into Eagle Brand mixture; chill 1-2 hours.

PREP TIME: 10 minutes
SERVINGS: 7 cups (1.7 L)

3 Pour into chilled bowl or serving cups. Garnish with nutmeg.

*Use only clean, uncracked eggs.

Frozen Bartender Parfaits

1 can (300 mL) **Regular or Low Fat Eagle Brand**®
1/3 cup (75 mL) Kahlua or other coffee-flavoured liqueur*
1 cup (250 mL) whipping cream, whipped

1 In large bowl, stir together Eagle Brand and liqueur. Fold in whipped cream.

2 Spoon 125 mL (1/2 cup) mixture into individual serving glasses. Freeze 3 hours or until firm.

3 Serve frozen, garnished as desired.

PREP TIME: 5 minutes
plus freezing time
SERVINGS: 6

*or Amaretto or other almond-flavoured liqueur.

Beverages

About Eagle Brand®

*E*agle Brand is an all-natural blend of whole milk and cane sugar condensed by a special vacuum-cooking process. The result is a rich, creamy-coloured, sweet milk which lends its properties to a wide variety of baked goods, desserts, confections and beverages. Evaporated milk is a non-sweetened product and cannot be substituted for Eagle Brand.

Eagle Brand comes in both regular and low fat formulations. Eagle Brand Low Fat sweetened condensed partially skimmed milk contains half the fat of regular Eagle Brand and performs the same as regular in most recipes. Both products are gluten free and certified kosher.

For more recipes...
www.eaglebrand.ca

Because it is pre-cooked and blended, Eagle Brand "magically" thickens with the addition of acid ingredients like lemon, orange or chocolate without cooking. And because most of the water has been removed, it also has a low freezing point, making it ideal for smoothly textured ice cream, without crystallization, again, without cooking. With the addition of heat, Eagle Brand creates luscious caramel, and based on the time heated, *you* control the consistency. Here are 3 ways to caramelize Eagle Brand. And remember, for safety's sake, to never heat Eagle Brand in the can.

Caramelizing Eagle Brand

OVEN METHOD   (1- 1 1/2 hours at 425°F (220°C)
Pour the contents of one can of Eagle Brand® into an 8 or 9" (20 or 23 cm) pie plate. Cover with foil and place in a larger shallow pan filled with hot water. Bake 1 to 1 1/2 hours, checking the water level in the pan from time to time, and refilling if necessary. The mixture does not require stirring. Bake until thick and light caramel-coloured. Then remove from the oven, and remove the foil. If desired, beat the warmed mixture until smooth. Cool and chill if desired.

STOVETOP METHOD   (1 1/2 hours)
Pour Eagle Brand® into top of double boiler; cover. Over low heat, simmer 1-1 1/2 hours or until thick and light caramel-coloured. Beat until smooth, if desired. Cool and chill if desired.

MICROWAVE METHOD   (14-18 minutes)
Pour Eagle Brand® into an 8 cup (2 L) glass measure. Cook, uncovered, at MEDIUM (50% power) 4 minutes, stirring after each 2 minutes. Reduce power to MEDIUM LOW (30%) and cook another 12-16 minutes, or until thick and light caramel-coloured, stirring briskly every 2 minutes until smooth. If desired, beat warm mixture until smooth. Cool and chill if desired.

Storage
Store leftovers covered and refrigerated for up to 1 week.